LIVE AN INSPIRED LIFE

By Using the Power of Your Subconscious

RAE-ANN
WOOD-SCHATZ

LIVE AN INSPIRED LIFE
By Using the Power of Your Subconscious

Copyright © 2011 by Rae-ann Wood-Schatz
ISBN 978-0-9864777-0-6

For more information, or to order additional copies of this book, please write to the publisher at:

Creators Code, Edmonton
10981 127th Street
Edmonton, Alberta T5M 0T1
rae-ann@creatorscode.com

Edited by Jordan Allan
Cover and book designed by Dominique Petersen

Printed in Canada

This book is written for anyone on the planet who feels compelled to live a more inspired life.

We live in turbulent times. A few years ago, I decided to stop following the news. Whenever it was on, it seemed like no matter what my vibration was prior to watching it, inevitably my vibration would drop. I would often feel defeated, overwhelmed and just plain sad. As I had already committed to living an inspired life, I decided that I would not only stop watching the news and reading the newspaper, but I would commit to a life-long journey of consciousness and congruence. It has been through that commitment that I have honestly stepped forward into living an inspired life. Now truthfully, there are still moments—sometimes even days—where I don't feel so inspired, but through my journey I have enough tools in my tool kit to support a shift and a step forward in my awareness.

It is my sincere desire that this book will serve as a source of understanding for anyone who is a kindred spirit and desires to live an inspired life. I hope that you can discover what may be keeping you from your dream and, more importantly, I hope to provide you with some tools that can quickly and easily be applied to help you stay on track.

Dedication

ACKNOWLEDGEMENTS

– Jay Fiset, my mentor, my guide, my inspiration and my number one butt kicker. Without you, this book and so many things in my life would never have been possible. I am forever grateful for the important role you have played in my life.

– Keith Hanna, my coach, my sounding board, my voice of reason in the face of insanity. Your wisdom has been instrumental to my success in living an inspired life.

– Lynda Howell, my best friend for life. It is how you live your life that has so often been a beacon of light for me in terms of how to open up to possibility.

– Rebekka Lehn, my friend, my right arm, my shoulder to cry on. Without you and your ongoing unconditional love and caring, my ability to move out of darkness and back into the light would be more arduous and life-force draining.

– My Personal Best family, to each and everyone of you that has worked with me, for me and alongside me, it has been your commitment to this work that has continued to not only inspire me, but you have been my most valuable teachers. Each and every time I step into the classroom, I learn something new about myself, about others and about humanity in general. A simple thank-you sounds insufficient, but thank-you nonetheless.

– Lastly and most importantly, my biological and chosen family. Jeffrey, for your patience and willingness to stand behind what I believe in even when it makes no sense to you personally. Jared,

Kenny and Jesse, for growing into such incredible human beings despite the fact I have spent so many hours away from home pursuing my dream. Nathan, for all the ways you mirror for me, and Quin, for loving me even when you don't have to. It is my solid footing in family that has allowed me to BE a greater version of myself.

TABLE OF CONTENTS

FOREWORD

Welcome to How to Live an Inspired Life. You are in for a treat—this is a book that can truly change your life. As the president of Personal Best Seminars Inc., I am honoured to write the foreword of *Live an Inspired Life*. Rae-ann and I have worked together for over a decade, and I am proud to call her a friend and business partner since 2002. I know what it is like to give birth to a book; in 2006, when I completed my best-selling book *Reframe Your Blame*, I spoke to Rae-ann and encouraged her to write her book, and I am thrilled that she did. Your life and mine will be better for it!

If you are reading this book, you are a seeker; you are on a path of growth and evolution and *Live an Inspired Life* will support you on your next step. Something you should know about the author is that she is one of the most engaged seekers I have had the privilege of working with over the past 22 years. You name it, she has done it and is probably certified to teach it! She has a Bachelor of Arts in Psychology, understands hypnosis and Neuro Linguistic Programming, is a Certified Shamanic Coach and much, much more. In Rae-ann you will find a kindred spirit, and by the end of this book, you will feel as though you know her and you will feel what those of us who really know Rae-ann feel—that she is one of those rare and amazing human beings who truly and genuinely care about you, your journey and your happiness.

As a conscious human being continuing to evolve, you know that the key to transformation isn't *knowing* but BEING, and this book will remind you how to BE inspired and inspiring for yourself, your family and the world. You will read real, authentic, personal examples that go to the core of transformation. One of the real gifts of this book is a glimpse into the process of waking up that Rae-ann so honestly shares with us. She provides a map and a template for each of us to dig deeper, let go of our limitations, push ourselves to be more in alignment with who we really are and ultimately live an inspired life.

Simply put, this book will change your life, so read on with and open heart, mind and soul. Ask yourself what your next level of application is and prepare yourself for a gift of transformation.

Enjoy!

Jay Fiset
President
Personal Best Seminars Inc.

INTRODUCTION

As an avid, lifelong learner, I can say from experience that although this book can provide you with tools that can easily be applied upon a first read, they must be consistently applied in order to stay on track long-term. My experience has taught me that to simply acquire knowledge and information is woefully inadequate when compared to what happens when knowledge becomes applied wisdom. In my practice, I have met many people who have come through either a counselling, coaching or seminar experience feeling alive, motivated and are excited about moving forward. I will run into them years later and when I ask them how they are doing, their response is often, "Fine, okay, I'm doing alright." Rarely do I hear them say, "I'm great, amazing! Let me tell you just how incredible I am." I believe this has everything to do with inconsistent application and a lack of ongoing support.

In my own life, I don't just read the latest and greatest self-help books: I have a coach, I have a mentor, and when I am not teaching in my classroom, I am in someone else's. In addition to support, I seek out opportunities for experiential learning wherever and whenever possible. Experiential learning is the experience of learning by doing. I use the analogy of learning to ride a bike. When you decided that you wanted to learn to ride a bike, did you head for the library and pick up a how-to book on bike riding? My guess is no. Did you seek out a workshop or seminar on bike riding to learn the process, not to mention have the experience of a dynamic facilitator who got you juiced and excited about how much fun and freedom you would have when you finally learned how to ride? Once again, my guess is no. Of course, you had some lessons and direction, perhaps even inspiration, from whoever was helping you, but your true learning came from the experience of bike riding. Most often, it is the experience of falling off and learning to make adjustments that ensures long-term, consistent success. This type of learning is so permanent that I trust that even if you have not ridden a bike for some time, you could easily pick one up and pedal for the stars. And more importantly, the fact that you've ridden a bike many times over means that your learning has deepened and solidified.

Similarly, think about the last motivational book you read: Do you recall feeling excited about what you were learning at the time, but upon reflection right now, can you honestly remember what the key lessons were and, most tellingly, which of those lessons, if any, you are applying with consistency today? While this book will give you the opportunity to learn something new and be reminded of some key concepts, the real challenge will come in using the tools with dedication and commitment. Like any good tool, it can only be put to use when it comes out of the tool box, otherwise it just sits and collects dust along with all the other tools in the shed.

The tools I will be introducing and using are pulled from a variety of sources and modalities. Some are from the practice of NLP (Neuro Linguistic Programming) and some are from hypnotherapy.

NLP is fundamentally the ability to understand how the mind (neuro), together with our use of language (linguistic), causes us to create mental systems that dictate how we think, feel and act (programming). My experience as an NLP practitioner has been centered predominantly around helping my clients uncover what drives them and giving them the tools they need to help rewrite what doesn't work. Sometimes I have been able to help them without ever engaging their conscious mind. It has also enabled me to get my children to clean their rooms without knowing why. Critics of NLP claim that, in the wrong hands, these techniques can be manipulative and unethical. I believe the operative phrase is "in the wrong hands," so I have been careful and mindful about using these techniques with integrity and with the sole intent of assisting people to live better, more powerful lives. The benefits of NLP are diverse and many. For the purposes of what we are doing here, the immediate benefits will be unlocking your mind and reframing beliefs and ideas that are keeping you from living an inspired life.

The lessons and understanding that I have learned through my practice as a hypnotherapist will allow me to explain how the subconscious mind works, why it functions the way it does and how important it is that you learn how your subconscious works so you can change what doesn't work and rewrite it to what does. Many people question why hypnosis works so well and even go so far as to wonder whether it is actually working or whether it is a fraud. My experience would suggest that, for whatever reason, hypnotherapy is one of the most powerful tools available to assist with leveraging the subconscious mind.

Hypnosis may be one of the most debated and controversial topics of modern medicine, but that doesn't mean that we can't get our facts straight. Before we delve further into our study of the subconscious mind and its twists and turns, let's establish where we're coming from first. Here are some of the most popular, yet unproven, takes on hypnosis:

- Many people assume that while they are in a state of hypnosis, they lose their ability to make proper moral decisions and that the hypnotherapist or hypnotist has control of their mind. In reality, if they are given a suggestion while in a hypnotic state that is counter intuitive, they will abreact and will often come up a level and engage their conscious mind. If you have ever witnessed stage hypnosis, you will notice periodically that the hypnotist will ask someone to leave the stage even after the show has begun. It is likely that the person would not accept the suggestion and came out of hypnosis and so was no longer a worthy candidate for the remainder of the show.

- Some people assume that they if they drop too deep into hypnosis, they won't be able to come out. This is a total myth and never has happened.

- Some people worry that hypnosis won't work and that they are wasting their time and energy attempting to use it as a support tool. The truth of the matter is that we have all been hypnotized on some level. If you have ever had the experience of driving home but don't remember the details of the drive home, you were in a mild disassociated state, which is a form of hypnosis. Also, when you daydream or when you seem oblivious to what is going on around you, you are in a mild state of hypnosis. Whether you can use it as a transformative tool has more to do with your trust in the process, your hypnotherapist and your desire.

I share some of the precepts here simply as a means for understanding the power of your mind. My experience would suggest that, for whatever reason, it is the decision-making part of the conscious mind that becomes timid when under a trance, which makes it "easier" for your mind to just automatically respond to the hypnotherapist's suggestions. Indeed, it will not hurt you to try hypnotism, and many of the other tools provided in this book will add value to your ability to leverage your conscious and subconscious mind to truly live an inspired life. Your destiny is still in your own hands.

The other tools I employ come from my work with Personal Best Seminars and what I have learned as a coach and a facilitator. I trust that nothing I share will be an original thought, so when I can speak to a source directly, I will; and when I speak from my experience, I will acknowledge in advance those people who have come before me, teaching and guiding others for decades.

For your part, I ask you to make a commitment before you continue to read this book; commit to finishing reading it no matter what distractions get in the way; commit to understanding yourself better and being more self-honest; and commit to making a life-change based on what you learn. Research suggests that only 10 percent of people really do want to change; the other 90 percent are content to live mediocre lives with mediocre results, and yet they will still feel victimized when they don't get what they say they dream about. They dream, but then don't do the necessary work. Commit to being part of the 10 percent that is truly committed to their dreams and to making the necessary changes to manifest what they desire and inevitably deserve. Be a rebel; push back against what doesn't work and push for what does.

Often I am asked the question: "So I really want a different life, and I really want to change. Some of the stuff going on in my life really sucks, but every time I try and do something different, it always seems to get screwed up. What am I doing wrong?" There are a few fundamental misconceptions in that question that are part of why people have a difficult time changing.

The first one is connected to the comment "I really want to change." What most people don't understand is that there is a delicate interplay between what we consciously say we want and what we really want at a "less-than-conscious" level. We tend to work only with the conscious part of our being, the part that is easily accessible and readily available in our thought process. However, the problem here is that the conscious part is really only about 10 percent of our thought process and only drives a 10 percent piece of our behavior—90 percent of what we believe sits at the less-than-conscious level. Chapter Two on Intention should help explain this.

The other part of this question that poses a challenge in terms of really supporting long-term change is the idea that "I don't like what I currently have going on and so I am motivated to change it." Again, this is an illusion. The truth is that you behave in the way that you do because it gives you some sort of payoff, and you have gotten used to getting that payoff by engaging in the behavior you now say you don't want. That payoff has become embedded in your belief system at the less-than-conscious level and is far more powerful and has a stronger impact on you than what you simply say you don't want. Chapter Three on Grungies and Payoffs should help put this into perspective.

One of the other things that has taken its fair share of motivated people to their knees is good, old procrastination. I have never met anyone—and I have met hundreds, maybe even thousands, of people—who has told me that they've never procrastinated. To truly be effective at long-term change, it is important to understand the role that procrastination plays in your life and, more importantly, how to deal with it. Chapter Five on Procrastination will give you a better idea of what I mean. The subsequent chapters will then help lay a foundation for change, and all I require is your willingness and commitment to long-term change.

Last but not least, I would like to define what living an inspired life means to me, and I encourage you to take the time to define it for yourself before you begin to read this book. The Canadian Oxford Dictionary defines inspired as:

1. stimulate or arouse (a person) to especially creative activity or moral fervour.
2. as if prompted by or emanating from a supernatural source; characterized by inspiration.

So, to put it simply, to live an inspired life simply means to feel aroused, animated and so filled with the drive and spirit to live your best life that you feel as if nothing can get in your way, especially not your subconscious mind and your dysfunctional ways of thinking, feeling and behaving; that you are not just the dream weaver, but you are the dream manifester; and that, when the day comes and you are about to cross over, you will honestly be able to say, "I didn't always do it great, but I did it with passion and consciousness."

Let us begin our journey together.

Your living is determined not so much by what life brings to you as by the attitude you bring to life; not so much by what happens to you as by the way your mind looks at what happens.

John Homer Miller

Chapter One:
RESULTS

Results are simply the outcomes that you have. Everything from the car you drive to the relationships you have, and everything in between, would be defined as results. You probably have some results in your life that you are particularly happy with, some that you are not really attached to one way or another, and truthfully some that are not bringing you joy or that you are particularly proud of.

Typical results that are notoriously attached to pain or stress are lack of money, relationships that aren't working, health or weight issues and time management challenges, just to name a few. Regardless of which results are for you, it is important that you begin to understand how we generate results, both those we are excited about and those we aren't.

HOW CONDITIONING IMPACTS OUR OUTCOMES

To help understand how we generate results, let's talk about how it is we attempt to change results when we decide there is value in having a particular outcome. When I began to study psychology, I took courses in classical and operant conditioning. Most people have heard of the experiments known as Pavlov's dogs. Essentially, what researchers were able to achieve with these dogs was a conditioned response to the sound of a bell and the association of the bell to the reward of food. To begin with, they would ring a bell just before offering food to the experimental canines. After a few rounds of this process, the researchers only needed to ring the bell to have the dogs start salivating in anticipation of receiving food. The concept of classical conditioning has some parallels in human behaviour, meaning that something that previously manifested as an unconditioned response can effectively be triggered, under certain conditions, to become a conditioned response.

This inevitably affects our results, but what is more relevant to our teaching here is the other psychological concept of operant conditioning. The theory behind operant conditioning is that if you can teach a behaviour, or even a series of behaviours, that ultimately result in a positive reward, the subject will repeat those behaviours consistently to ensure the reward; or conversely, if someone is exhibiting a response that is maladaptive, that behaviour can be extinguished through consequence. As a student, I was given the task of teaching a rat and a guinea pig to go through multiple steps involving levers and pulleys to get to a food pellet at the end. In fact, the guinea pig was willing to remember and perform six different steps to get to the reward. It was also possible to have the rat or guinea pig perform those functions by emitting a loud noise into the cage and not stopping it until the subject performed the requisite behaviour.

So, to make an analogy with human behaviour, we could say that if someone were to change their behaviour in such a way that it brought about a positive outcome, they would probably be quite consistent in enacting that change to guarantee the ongoing positive result or reward. Or, at the opposite end of the continuum, it means that if someone behaved in a certain way and associated the subsequent negative result to that specific behaviour, they would more than likely not repeat the same behaviour.

So let's continue with the use of analogies to assist with our understanding. For example, if we were to use the concept of operant conditioning to explain the rationale behind dieting, the idea would be: I change my behaviour in regard to food and exercise, I eat less, I work out, I lose weight, I not only look great and have better self esteem, but I have more energy and feel amazing. There are already multiple positive reinforcements. So conceptually, I should be thin forever. Adding further reinforcement, I am aware that if I don't change my habits, I may cause myself significant long-term health issues like a heart attack or diabetes. Either way, I am motivated to maintain the change and continue dieting. But somehow, based on the results, this schema never plays out exactly as science predicts; my weight varies and is often on the side of being somewhat overweight.

It didn't take long for those tasked with understanding human behaviour to determine that there was a missing link in these conditioning concepts and theories. So next came the idea of working on attitudes. We have all heard the cliché "are you a cup-half-full person or a cup-half-empty person?" This phrase typifies the practice of encouraging people to change their mental attitudes, stressing that if you have the "right" attitude, you will naturally make the "right" choices in regard to your behaviours, thereby creating the "right" results.

Let's return to our diet metaphor. If you were a television watcher in the 1990s, you may remember the "ParticipACTION" advertisements. The makers of those ads were attempting to get people excited (an attitude) about exercising. I suppose that if I could see the benefit in having fun and keeping fit, I would be less stressed and happier. Thus, if I had the right attitude about exercise, I would naturally be inclined to do it more. I don't know about you, but I distinctly remember changing the channel when the ParticipACTION ads came on. I certainly don't remember getting up off the couch and going for a run.

HOW LAW OF ATTRACTION PLAYS A ROLE

In recent times, North America has been exposed to the concept of the law of attraction. Now, although this is not a new idea, it has never before received so much attention. The law of attraction is built on the premise of beliefs and attitude; if I frame my life and focus positively on the outcomes that I want to create, then I will call it, or "will" it, into existence. Wallace D. Wattles, in his book *The Science of Getting Rich*, explains:

There is a thinking stuff from which all things are made, and which, in its original state, permeates, penetrates, and fills the interspaces of the universe.

A thought, in this substance, produces the thing that is imaged by the thought.

Man can form things in his thought, and, by impressing his thought upon formless substance, can cause the thing he thinks about to be created.

In order to do this, man must pass from the competitive to the creative mind; he must form a clear mental picture of the things he wants, and hold this picture in his thoughts with the fixed PURPOSE to get what he wants, and the unwavering FAITH that he does get what he wants, closing his mind to all that may tend to shake his purpose, dim his vision, or quench his faith.

That he may receive what he wants when it comes, man must act NOW upon the people and things in his present environment.

I have had many people come through my classroom who have said that they've been working with this idea of the law of attraction, but it just doesn't seem to be working the way the movies or the books said it would. Again, this is evidence that there is still a missing link.

THE REAL SECRET IS IN UNDERSTANDING MY BELIEF SYSTEM

Which brings us to the third and probably most impactful contributor to how we create results—our belief system. Think of your belief system as your blueprint or your map of reality. It is the lens through which you filter everything in your world. What you believe about yourself, others or the world will inevitably impact how you feel, your attitude and ultimately will determine how you act or behave.

You were not born with your belief system; in fact, some would say you were just a blank slate waiting to be written on. *Tabula Rasa* is the name of epistemological thesis that believes individuals are born without built-in mental content and that the totality of their knowledge comes from experience and perception. This has lead to much debate and research on the power of nature versus nurture. While there is much data to support the nature camp, such as twin studies and hereditary experiments, one must admit that, regardless of what nature provides us with from the beginning, nurture also has significant impact. When we realize this fact, we can then begin to see how important awareness of what those "nurturing influences" were so we can properly identify what has become our belief system and, more importantly, our primary navigational system guiding us through our lives.

There are a number of studies that link certain body issues with emotional stressors and experiences that have created certain beliefs. For example, a physician by the name of Edgar A. Barnett wrote a book entitled *Unlock Your Mind and Be Free*. In this wonderful book, he identifies five body syndromes and explains in detail what the issue in the body is and what the corresponding emotional causes are:

1. The first body syndrome is the *crying syndrome* and covers the parts of the body from the solar plexus upwards: the chest, the shoulders, the head and the back of the neck. The cause of the crying syndrome is one's inability to make a decision, either because the person is relying on someone else's action or because of past beliefs and conditioning. Headaches are the most common manifestation as the frustration of not making a decision causes the muscles in the scalp to tighten and throb painfully. The crying syndrome can become so severe that it causes a migraine headache. Other symptoms include watery eyes, sinus congestion, canker sores and grinding of the teeth.

2. The second syndrome is the *responsibility syndrome*. The bodily areas that are affected are the upper back, shoulders and upper spinal areas. The psychological causes are the

proverbial carrying the weight of the world on your shoulders, feeling overburdened, or not willing to be responsible for choices and things in your life. The physiological response is a tightness of the back and shoulders and, when certain movements occur, this cramping can cause pain or damage to the affected areas.

3. The third syndrome is the *sexual frustration* or *guilt syndrome*. The affected areas are the stomach, groin and lower back. The psychological causes are religion-based scripting causing guilt, sexual frustrations, feelings of sexual inadequacy or guilt for cheating. Physically, this can manifest as stomach issues, constipation, acidity, excessive menstrual cramps or bleeding, vaginal or bladder infections, prostrate issues and kidney trouble.

4. The fourth syndrome is the *fight* or *reaching syndrome*. The body areas affected are the arms, hands and fingers. The psychological cause is the need to express and at the same time not being willing to reach for the need due to feelings of inadequacy and a lack of self worth. This creates feelings of deep rejection due to the perception of unattainable goals. Physiologically, it manifests as extremely hot or cold hands, warts or blisters on those extremities, or arthritis.

5. The fifth syndrome is the *flight syndrome* and affects the body area from the thighs to the feet. It signifies the need to run or escape, either physically or emotionally. The psychological connection is grounded in the fear of facing certain situations out of a fear of success or fear that the situation will be to painful or boring. Physiologically, it can manifest as blistering on the toes or the feet, or poor circulation, or leg pain.

Louise Hay, author of *You Can Heal Your Life*, carries these ideas even further and has a complete glossary of physical issues and their corresponding emotional, or belief, connection. As you can see, there is ample research and evidence to support the theory that what we think or how we feel about the things in our external world is impacting our internal world, and so therefore, conceptually speaking, these attitudes will cycle back outward and no longer be just affecting our results but in fact be determining them.

So let us consider how our perceptions and subsequently our belief systems came into being.

Who do you think had the greatest impact on the evolution of your map of reality? Your parents, of course. How many times have you done something, been triggered by something, or stood behind or against a concept or idea and, when someone asked you why you were so adamant, you simply answered that it was what your parents taught you to believe?

Now, keep in mind that some of what your parents taught you to believe has supported you. Perhaps it has helped you to live a more moral life, or helped you to have the confidence to take risks and to go after what you want—you know what is true for you. The other reality is that there is likely some stuff that has accumulated in there that has limited or blocked you in some way. Perhaps you were told that you weren't very smart in a particular area and so have never pushed yourself to take risks in that area as you have already decided you will fail. Or perhaps you were told that you were bad at something, and "magically" you seem to continue to have negative experiences that have reinforced that negative belief and made it seem true.

Let me give you a couple of examples from my own life. I was told from a very early age that my father was critical and unhappy when I was born female. I had an older sister, and my guess is that somewhere in the evolution of my father's belief system, he felt it was important that he have a son. So based on what I was told, I decided there must be something wrong with my gender. My little girl mind then deduced that for me to gain my father's approval, I would need to somehow be the son he didn't get when I was born. If you look at photographs of me as a child, it was painfully obvious that I was a girl truly walking the "tomboy" walk.

In fact, I remember a trip my family took in 1974, when we traveled to Spokane, Washington, for the World's Fair. We were in a restaurant, and I needed to use the restroom. My mom told me to ask the waiter where the washroom was. I approached the fellow behind the counter, and he absentmindedly pointed towards a nearby door. I went inside and imagine my surprise when I saw a man standing at a urinal! Not only was I horrified and embarrassed, but I interpreted and filtered that event from the perspective of being judged and misunderstood. I didn't consciously decide that I wanted to be a boy; I just wanted to be accepted by my dad and somehow, at a less than conscious level, it related to my belief he wanted a son.

In addition to unconsciously choosing to look like a boy, I excelled in sports and all of my closest friends were boys. One time, when I was 11 years old and out playing a game of street hockey, my mother came out and instructed me to put on a shirt. When I asked her why, considering it was very hot out and we were playing hard, she replied that my body was no longer like the body of my peers and that my being shirtless was totally unacceptable and inappropriate.

This was another reinforcement for me that being female was bad and wrong, and I even started feeling angry at my body. Fundamentally, this began the process of not just wanting to be more like a boy, but also hating being a girl. You can imagine how having this belief instilled at an early age affected my femininity, my self-esteem and my self worth. Every time I looked in the mirror, especially as I reached puberty, I was reminded of how bad and wrong I was, and the circle of self hate had already started, and none of it because anyone had told me directly that I was unacceptable or unworthy! It was the genesis of my developing belief system.

In fact, in Edgar Barnett's book *Unlock Your Mind and Be Free*, he employs the metaphor of a prison and writes about the many ways our mind imprisons us. He ties our imprisonment back to a series of what he calls our "perceived crimes." In my example, he would say that I performed the "crime" of being born the wrong gender. Barnett also gives a number of other examples that I am sure many of you can relate to, crimes like being wrong for just being here. If you ever were told you were a "mistake" and that your parents weren't ready to have a child—you created a shotgun wedding scenario or whatever the story may be—you may feel guilty for just being on the planet. Or perhaps you suffer from the guilt of having committed the "crime" of being angry, or afraid, or hurt, or happy, or curious; somewhere along the way, you were criticized or condemned for expressing these emotions, so you repressed them and felt guilty for even having them.

Nonetheless, I am sure you can see the potential price one would pay inside their own minds and in their external worlds for the perception of being guilty of one of these "crimes". You can also see what type of belief system this could create and what the ripple effect of that belief could subsequently be.

WHAT DO YOU BELIEVE?

Consider for a moment what some of those deep-seated, childhood-created beliefs are for you. More importantly, consider what their impact on you might still be. If you have difficulty remembering significant events from your childhood, simply consider what results you have today that you carry negative energy on. Think about what the belief might be that causes you to create that result, and then work backwards and see if you can connect that to a childhood event. If you are still struggling, consider the value in seeing a trained hypnotherapist who could take you through a "regression process," where you can discover in a hypnotic state the root cause of the "presenting issue." Also know that if you can't remember what the "sponsoring event" is, it really doesn't matter in the larger scheme of things. What does matter is that you begin to understand that any result you currently have in your life stems back and is anchored in your belief system, and just requires a process of writing over the old script that does not work any longer.

Now you must also understand that beliefs don't come singularly. You have many, perhaps hundreds, of beliefs and, as you move through life and have more and more experiences, the beliefs that are similar will attach to and reinforce one another. Eventually, you will have amassed some significant core beliefs that pepper many others. It's also possible that you will engender a set of beliefs that seem to contradict another set. The result can sometimes be a feeling of incongruence and frustration, manifesting as confusion, a lack of clarity and the experience of feeling stuck.

Another example from my life relates back to my childhood and knowing that my father didn't want me based on my gender. I already mentioned that I worked hard to gain his approval by trying to be something I wasn't. Now here comes the twist. First off, my father was very much a man; he only did men's work and did nothing that would traditionally resemble women's work. In fact, when my mother was hospitalized with a hysterectomy, all we ate that week was bacon and eggs. It was the only thing my dad knew how to cook. I also remember the first time I saw him doing the dishes—I couldn't help but wonder what was wrong with him.

Part of my dad's masculinity came from his athleticism. As a child, I don't remember consciously thinking that perhaps if I was athletic too, my dad might finally decide I was okay after all; but based on results, it was just another attempt at acceptance. When I was 10 or 11 years old, my dad was in the habit of running a couple miles every day. Before I went to sleep one evening, I decided that I would go running with him in the morning. I met him at the door dressed and ready to go. He looked puzzled and asked me what I was doing. I told him my plan to run with him. He shrugged, sighed a little, and off we went.

My dad was a seasoned runner, so of course he was much larger and more fit than I was. We weren't too far into the run when he stopped and, with a frustrated tone, told me to go home because I was slowing him down. Picture me, blood rushing, heart racing, legs bursting with pain, little cheeks flushed, breathless, thinking (on a deeper level) that I will show him, he will love me, I will show him, he will love me, with each pounding step—only to then, once again, be told that I was inadequate and I should just go home.

Now you might think that I would have just given up the fight and surrendered to a life of worthlessness and been done with it. But what my father also taught me to be was tenacious. He is one of the most tenacious, stubborn people I know. So, not totally discouraged, I woke up the next day and decided to ride my bike alongside my dad to make sure I was going fast enough to keep up with him. I met him at the door, bike poised and ready. His expression said "Oh God, not again," and he silently started running with me pedaling frantically behind him. I rode with fury and finally had the feeling of doing something important with my dad. However, the feeling of pride and accomplishment only lasted for a split second. He suddenly stopped running and, with that same look of exasperation I was used to seeing, he told me to go home since the next leg of his run took him to places my bike would not easily go.

As I stood straddling my bike and watched him run away, it was like a part of my belief system underwent a radical shift. In fact, it was in that moment that I decided this whole being-a-boy thing sucked and that all boys—my dad being the exemplar—were just insensitive jerks, boorish, piggish and just plain ignorant. I share this story not only to point out how beliefs can evolve, but will later use it to show what the impact of this belief was on my life and my relationships as I grew older and became an adult.

Other than your parents, the other contributors to your belief system are your teachers, peers, religion and, especially in this day and age, the media. The numbers vary, but on average we are bombarded by somewhere between 1500 and 3000 messages and advertisments a day. As an example, I want you to think about your first experience of alcohol. Do you remember thinking to yourself that it was the most amazing experience you ever had and could hardly wait for the next opportunity? If not, why would you seek out the drunken experience again? Perhaps you saw the Budweiser commercial that depicted just how much fun life could be when alcohol was part of it. Either way you look at it, the media impacts the choices you make, how you feel about certain things and certainly how you move through your life and the world.

It is thought that your core belief system—how you filter the world, the lens through which you view everything—is primarily in place by the time you are 12 years old. So essentially, when you make decisions, those choices are framed from the perspective of a 12 year old. Again, on some level that may work and support you, but on another level, it most certainly may not.

HOW YOUR EGO PLAYS A PART

So why is it that we have a belief system as opposed to our animal brothers and sisters, who rely on making decisions more from instinct than from learned behaviour? The truth is that it has everything to do with the reality that we are also the only species with an ego. And it is because we have an ego that we are at the mercy of our beliefs.

But don't worry—it's not all bad. Your belief system has kept you safe and is an important part of your survival. For example, if you put your hand on a hot stove and it burnt you, you will likely not make the same mistake again. No one had to say, "Pull your hand away, that is hurting." You have instinct and then a belief that says stoves are hot and dangerous. When you learned to cross the street, someone instilled you with the belief that it's important to wait until it is safe to cross, again a belief that keeps you safe.

The bad news is there is another part of your belief system that does not serve you quite as well. It is the part of your belief system that wants desperately to be right about what it has decided is true. Consider for a moment when you are engaged in an argument; you are involved in the argument because you are quite convinced that you are right, but the other person who is arguing against you also believes that they are right. The truth is that reality is subjective and, depending on how attached to being right you are, you may just blow out your relationships by acting stubborn and convicted. Consider what often happens at a four-way stop. How many times have you seen people—or maybe you've even done this yourself—risk life and limb to show the other person that they were right. They got there first!

Eckert Tolle, in his book *The New Earth*, has attempted to help us understand our ego better and how to mature it. In fact, in a blog response to a question a reader posted about how to better understand what the ego is, he replied with the following statement:

The ego is a stage in the evolution of human consciousness. It is not your enemy. To perceive somebody or something as an enemy is in fact one of the main misperceptions or delusions of the egoic unconsciousness. So, you cannot fight against the ego and win that fight. If you think you have won the fight against the ego, it is the ego in you that thinks so and it has enlarged itself. So the ego is not an enemy, but a dysfunction. Looked at from one point of view, it is an entity that the mind created. From another perspective, however, it is simply a delusion, resulting in a distorted way of perceiving reality and consequently in dysfunctional behaviour. This second perspective is probably a more helpful one.

A delusion dissolves when you recognize it as delusion, and so does the ego. The ego is the by-product, as it were, of the rapid development of our faculty of thought over the past 6000 years. We lost ourselves in thought, that is to say became identified with it to such an extent that we now derive our sense of who we are from thinking. Thought is a particular way for universal intelligence to express itself. It is no more than a tiny aspect of that vast intelligence. Thought, through naming things, analyzes, dissects, and separates reality into bits and pieces. Thinking can be a helpful practical tool, but when you identify with thinking, the delusion of separation arises.

Your reality becomes fragmented. You lose your original sense of connectedness with Being ("paradise"). You become unhappy, needy, discontented, full of ever unfulfilled desire, and you are always unconsciously attempting to regain your lost sense of being, of who you are.

Life is one and I am one with all life.

When you know this truth, the ego dissolves. To know means to realize. How, then, do you realize this truth?

At this moment – the only moment there is – there are some thoughts moving across your mind (the words you are reading and whatever your mind is adding to them). However, you can also KNOW that these thoughts are moving across your mind. That knowing is the dimension of awareness. It has nothing to do with thinking. While thinking happens, you can know yourself as the aware-ness behind the thinking, the alert stillness in the back-ground – ungraspable, indefinable, elusive.

When you disidentify from thinking, you may also discover a growing ability within you to perceive things and people without immediately naming them. In this way, the ego, which is the unconscious habit of identifying with every thought that arises, begins to dissolve.

So in effect our ego is fundamental part, if not the essence, of our belief system and until we can disidentify from it, it will continue to drive our results and will anchor us to that perpetual need to be right.

HOW WANTING TO BE RIGHT CAN HURT

It is this desire to be right that is the part of a belief system and an ego that can often be the challenge and antithesis to living an inspired life.

Let's go back to my story and analyze my decision, made during a critical time of my belief system's development, that men were essentially pigs. Now, if you trust that part of the purpose of the belief system's job is to be right, it makes sense that you will naturally—likely at a less-than-conscious level—attract people, experiences and events into your life to reinforce that belief. So, as a child, I decided that men are pigs, but now let's fast forward into my adulthood.

When I met my future husband, I fell madly in love. Now, also around the time I met him, I decided that I wanted to shed my good-girl image and push my independence. He was a bad boy who quit school, drank and partied all the time, worked on the pipeline, made lots of money and had every girl in town after him. At 16 years old, I moved out of my parent's house and moved in with him and two of his buddies. It didn't take long before the novelty of being with a bad boy wore off, and I found myself miserable and lonely. I was second to Old Vienna beer; not just sometimes, but all the time. So life, as I was living it, was beginning to show me that I was right about the whole men-are-pigs thing.

Around this same time, I enrolled in university. I decided after a year of general studies that psychology seemed like a reasonable choice; after all, I had a belief that said that I am good at helping people—in fact, my dad called me Ann Landers ever since I can remember. Post degree, I was working in a nightclub wondering what would come next in my life. My partner was full-on into his addiction, and I was feeling pretty lost in my direction and not very happy overall.

One evening, I was working behind the main bar and a woman came over, sat down and ordered a drink. We chatted as she waited for her date to show up, and I wasn't very busy. As it turned out, she was the volunteer coordinator at a local women's shelter. She suggested that perhaps I might want to try volunteering to explore that side of psychology and human services. I called the next day and, after a short stint as a volunteer, I had my first real job helping people.

Now remember, my belief system told me that men are pigs, and my first significant job was in a women's shelter. Can you see how I now had even more evidence that my belief was right? In fact, not only was the evidence all around me, but I was reading massive amounts of literature and scientific studies about misogynists, which for the most part solidified my belief about men.

Jump ahead to June 13, 1988: I am in the hospital enduring what was becoming almost 14 hours of labor. Finally, my baby went into distress, not being able to endure labor any longer. They put me under anesthetic, and when I woke up hours later in pain and disoriented, they congratulated me and told me that I had a healthy baby boy. I have to be honest—my heart sank. How was it possible that I, Rae-ann Wood-Schatz, man hater, could have possibly given birth to a boy? Was karma punishing me for something bad I had done in a past life? My alcoholic husband, of course, was quite proud. "Can't have too many pigs on the planet" was his perspective, and he bragged about his prowess of having produced a son.

I continued along my life journey, feeling victimized and frustrated while raising a young boy, jealous of my friends who were having girls. I was miserable and unhappy, going to work every day and being reminded of how just unfair the world is. On June 27, 1993, I was back in hospital, struggling to give birth the natural way. Again I was put under anesthetic, and again I woke up to the shocking news of the birth of another boy.

Now, I want you to consider the impact that the belief I had about men was having on my life and my relationship with my sons. By the time my third son came along, I had begun the process of waking up and realized that, for me to be successful as a wife and mother, I had better begin the process of re-working my old belief. I stopped working in the family violence arena, I left my husband and I actively began to seek out new evidence to contradict the belief I had previously held.

To be honest, however, I still struggle with that old belief. It shows up every now and again when one of my sons—who are reaching adulthood now—do something that I judge and criticize, because it is easy for me to associate their behaviour with their gender and nothing else. But the truth is that I will be forever grateful for having the opportunity to discover the belief existed and to begin the process of rewriting and re-patterning.

In future chapters, I will talk more about how to change beliefs that are not serving you. What is important now is that you begin to understand just how powerful our beliefs are in manifesting feelings and behaviours, and if you ever hope to change behaviour that doesn't work, you need to become aware of what your belief system is dictating in your life. Suffice it to say, you do have beliefs that support you, but you have just as many, likely even more, that are blocking you from living an inspired life. The gift is in knowing that everything you believe you have learned, and because of that, it is also true that you can unlearn what doesn't work and relearn something more powerful.

To begin the process of unlearning, you must first become aware. To become aware, you must begin by telling yourself the truth. Again, look at your results, those you like and those you don't, and consider what beliefs you have that would cause those results to manifest. Find a process that can experientially bring you to the brink of understanding your belief system. Take a Personal Best seminar or something like it—there are programs out there designed to help you make the unconscious conscious. See a hypnotherapist, and you will realize that you truly deserve and are worthy of living an inspired life.

Chapter Two:
INTENTION

In one of my workshops, I ask participants to define what they think "intention" means. I get varied responses, but most people recognize that it is related to goal setting, about deciding something and then getting busy manifesting or bringing that decision into fruition. The Canadian Oxford Dictionary defines intention as: "a thing intended; an aim or purpose." Essentially, the base principle is the same whether it was a client's definition or a textbook definition—intention means to set a plan and then get after it. In reality, though, those definitions fall short of the truth and failed or thwarted intentions are often the reason people get frustrated, when they don't get what they had intended to create.

Let's go back to the concept of the law of attraction. In the last chapter, we addressed how the law of attraction, as presented in the literature, was misrepresented by the idea of only needing to change how you think, be positive about it and it will manifest—simple as that. This is where understanding "intention" at a deeper level is critical, and is often not well explained in the law of attraction teachings.

A NEW WAY OF THINKING ABOUT INTENTION

The drawing of the iceberg on the following page should help put this into perspective. Picture the iceberg as a representation of the mind of a typical human being with the ability to think critically. The top half of the iceberg represents your consciousness, about 10 percent; the symbols inside the tip represent your beliefs. When I say consciousness, I am talking about your beliefs that you are actually aware of and can be easily articulated. Remember, you have beliefs that support you and beliefs that limit you—both of these beliefs are a part of the tip.

I have been conscious for quite some time that I used to have a belief that all men are pigs, so that belief would show up in the tip of my iceberg. I am also aware that I have a belief that says I am tenacious, and when I put my mind to something, I get what I want. This belief has supported me in many different ways over the course of my life, and I am very aware that it has been a conscious belief for decades. It too would exist at the tip of my iceberg.

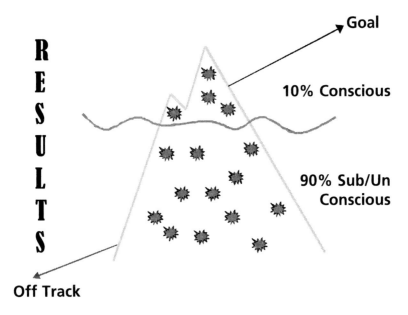

Let's talk a little bit more about the conscious and the less than conscious, keeping in mind that it is the less-than-conscious parts of your mind—making up 90 percent of the iceberg—that become a critical part of your work if you ever hope to truly live an inspired life. Consciousness could truly be the last important subject still beyond the grasp of our full understanding. What we have discovered as we continue to evolve is that there are levels of awareness, that we not only have thoughts that are available to our thinking mind, but thoughts that are arising and influencing us from places that we're not able to grasp with our conscious mind. The lower half of the iceberg represents your less than conscious, and the symbols in the lower half represent your beliefs that are buried or hidden from your conscious self.

HOW INTENTION MANIFESTS AS RESULTS

So where do your results come from? Most people assume it is from their conscious thoughts—because again, isn't that what the law of attraction teaches us? What you believe, you achieve; what you focus on, you create. While there is wisdom and truth in those clichés, the problem is that it is the less-than-conscious part of what you believe that gets overlooked and is the direct cause of the skewed results. In this way, results come from both the conscious and the less than conscious.

Take a moment now and find a piece of paper and a pen. Spend a few minutes and write out what your intention is in relationship to your health, your financial picture and your relationships with others. Keep this handy as we will be coming back to it.

Let's use a tangible example. Let's say that you decide you are consciously sick and tired of being broke all the time and that you intend to change your fortunes by increasing your annual income to $100,000 a year. Looking at our iceberg metaphor, you consciously set the goal at $100,000.

You get busy over the course of the year investing and working a second job. When you are part way through the year, you realize that you have only managed to manifest $40,000. You are off track with what you consciously said you wanted to create. If you look at the diagram, you will notice that "off track" is sitting below the line, in the less than conscious. So if we trust this idea that it is our beliefs that drive our feelings and our actions, then we can assume that it must be our less-than-conscious beliefs that are causing the intended outcome to fall short. Perhaps you have beliefs like "I don't deserve to make that much money," or "I am not capable of being that successful," or even "Money is the source of all evil, and by making that much money, I may invite evil into my life." Remember that these beliefs are not conscious—you are not even aware they exist; but based on the result of making less than $100,000, there is something happening that is blocking or stopping you from getting what you consciously said you intended to create.

So you get to the end of the year, and you have made $75,000. I ask again: What was your intention? If you said $100,000, you are in illusion. However, if you said $75,000, you are bang on. Your intention, regardless of what you said when the year began, was to make $75,000. How do we know? Because that is what you made. In this manner, if what you consciously say you want and what you get are out of alignment, then it is your less-than-conscious beliefs that are inevitably impacting your intentions.

What hasn't changed in any of this is the reality that you are intending to have every result you have in your life, both the ones you like and, more tellingly, the ones you don't like. So, conscious or unconscious, it is exactly your intention to have the car you drive, the partner you have, the house you have, the job you have, the weight you are; whatever the result is. How do I know? Because it is what it is. Now you might be saying, "No way! My car is breaking down, my relationship sucks, I hate my job, and my self esteem has tanked because of my weight—and you think that I want to have that in my life?"

Well, yes, at some level you do, and if the results you currently have are those that, at a conscious level, make you unhappy, again you have to begin to pull the less than conscious into the conscious if you ever hope to rewrite your beliefs and live a life of joy and inspiration.

What is important at this stage is an honest evaluation of what your true intent is, and the truth lies in the current experience of your results. So go back to the list you created earlier about your intentions in terms of health, wealth and relationships and, armed with your new knowledge about intention, write about the truth of what it is you intend in those areas. For example, I intend to live paycheck to paycheck, I intend to have relationships that are hard and filled with conflict, I intend to carry 20 extra pounds; whatever is true for you, you must be willing to put it down on paper.

If you are feeling a little discouraged, I understand. Sometimes the truth hurts; in fact, there is a quote by David Gerald in *Rage for Revenge* that reads, "The truth will set you free, but first it will piss you off." Staying in self-deception may seem safer on some level, but inevitably it will be the thing that keeps you stuck where you are; and if where you are is less than joyful, then start with the truth and be willing to work from there. Remember that changing patterns and beliefs that don't work starts with awareness. Then you can start finding strategies to change those beliefs that are self-limiting. When you begin to understand how intention really works—it is not only about the conscious declaration or goals you have set, but also about what you believe at a less-than-conscious level—you are then in a better position to leverage this understanding and use the concept of intention to its full advantage, helping you get what it is you say you want. Chapter Nine on Faith should help to clarify this point.

Chapter Three:
GRUNGIES AND PAYOFFS

Grungies are the negative emotions we carry around and the subsequent ways we act in response to those negative emotions. The cause of our negative feelings is as diverse as we are. Something that would cause me to react in a particular way could cause a totally different feeling or reaction in you. The point is that there are certain events that will trigger certain feelings in you. Some of these feelings you will consider to be positive, some you will label as negative.

When you can identify the positive feelings, you can naturally take action to seek out opportunities to elicit more of those experiences and the subsequent feelings that you enjoy—this is an opportunity for you to move closer to living a more inspired life. When people begin to question their purpose in life and begin their journey toward mastery, taking note of the things that make you happy is a fundamental part of building your self-awareness. However, it is the things that you feel the most negative about, or the things you do that cause you pain, that carry exponential weight in regard to pulling you off track. So it is important we spend this chapter examining these grungies.

Having worked with people for the better part of my adult life, the chart on the following page lists what would be considered typical grungie emotions for many people.

MARTYR	BOREDOM	PAIN
RESENTMENT	FRUSTRATION	CONFUSION
SICKNESS	HUMILIATION	DEPRESSION
TIREDNESS	VICTIMIZATION	SELF-PITY
JEALOUSY	FEAR	SADNESS
DISAPPOINTMENT	SUFFERING	ENVY
EMBARRASSMENT	ANGER	GUILT
WORTHLESSNESS	WORRY	ANXIETY

Part of personal development is learning what your triggers are so that you can begin to get some control over how you react to those events that elicit your grungie response. It is also important to learn how you participate in setting those events up. You must begin to recognize and tell the truth about what your main grungies are, and, more importantly, you must understand why those grungies are still present in your life.

One of the primary reasons that they are still around is because, somewhere along the way, you acted in a certain way and you got a certain payoff for that behaviour. So, at some level, every time you act that way, you are seeking out that payoff or are working to reinforce the belief you created when you got the payoff the first time.

Let's look at a couple of examples from the chart.

ANGER AS A GRUNGIE

Let's start with anger. All human beings have experienced anger. Even if you don't remember when you were a baby, I am sure you have been around a baby and have seen them act angry. Consider for a moment what a baby wants when he or she is angry. Usually it is a desire to have food, comfort or a diaper change. If you are a parent, or have been around a parent, what happens when a baby gets angry? Typically, the parents jump into action to care for whatever the baby needs.

Now, fast-forward into adulthood: When you get angry, what payoff do you think you are seeking? Likely, just like when you were a baby, you are hoping to manipulate the person who is the receiver of your anger. You want them to do or say something, and you will stay puffy and angry until you have gotten your way. Now, depending on your beliefs about anger, how angry you get and what your anger looks like will be different. But the bottom line is the same—you are attempting to manipulate someone into doing something. How long you stay angry will also vary depending on your belief system.

The other reality is that sometimes you don't get what you want—the payoff isn't the same as when you were a baby—and again, depending on your belief system, you may shift to using a different grungie, like victimization or pouting, or you may just shift to a different emotion all together. My partner Jeff is a good example of someone who is not quick to anger, but when he gets angry, he gets very puffy. When he doesn't get what he wants, however, his anger gradually subsides, and in fact, he will often then try being nice to see if he can get any further than when he was attempting to use anger.

I have especially noticed that the longer he stays with me and the older our kids get (we have five sons, ranging in age from 15 to 22), he is even less quick to anger and far less likely to get stuck in his anger for very long. I believe that he has never really been successful at manipulating me with his anger, and so the law of diminishing returns suggests that the more times he goes without the payoff, the less attractive that response becomes. I am not sure how his ex-wife used to be with him, but my guess is she responded to his anger and he got some of what he wanted, so he learned that, even though there was a price to pay in his relationship (in this case, divorce), he still got something and hence the behaviour continued and carried forward into his relationship with me.

Children will often react and do what a parent wants when they get angry. In fact, some parents have this down to such a science that they don't even have to get angry anymore; they just have to threaten to get angry and the child will jump into action. In the case of our children, Jeff had been able to get some of what he wanted with anger, but as the boys got older, they pushed back more frequently and with more tenacity. I have, on more than one occasion, seen the fight for the alpha position intensify to the point where anger is the sole energy between both Jeff and one of our sons. The end result varies, but as time goes on and the payoff of using anger starts shifting to the boys—as Jeff backs down from a fight, defeated—the unfortunate reinforcement of getting-what-I-want-by-being-angry is moving to our sons. I fear the consequences as they move into adulthood and will likely continue to attempt to use anger to get what they want in other relationships.

Based on my understanding of how anger ultimately doesn't work in relationships, I have attempted to 'manipulate' our children using a different method. The desired outcome is often not that different than Jeff's, but I have learned a more direct approach than the grungie route. For example, when I desire a certain action or behaviour from one of my children and they ignore me or even push back, I find that confiscating their cell phone is enough to get them to do what I want. Don't get me wrong; there is usually still drama attached to the experience, but it doesn't go on for long and, so long as I stay calm and convicted until they realize that no matter how angry they get they are not getting what they want, compliance and progress usually follows.

Now you might be thinking, "Well, that is fine with children, but what about when you have a relationship with an adult who attempts to manipulate you with anger and you aren't really in a position to take away their cell phone?" The truth is that we don't control anyone, adult or child, and in fact we can only have 100 percent control over three things and three things only: our beliefs, our attitudes and our behaviours. Jay Fiset, in his book *Reframe Your Blame*, takes this idea to a much deeper level and I encourage you to read his book for further enlightenment. In terms of what we're discussing here, he would say that I may think I am controlling my children when I take their cell phone, but the truth is they ultimately are making the choice to comply not because I have power over them, but because, for them, a life without text messaging is like a life without air. They will ultimately make the choice to do whatever I ask them to do just to get what they want, which in this case is their cell phone back. So, in the end, we have engaged in the dance of manipulating each other, and as long as we both get what we want, we remain happy in our dance.

Let us go back to the idea of anger and adult relationships. The concept is the same as with teenagers, or anyone you have a relationship with: Both people want something, and we only get angry when we think things should be a certain way and how they are seems out of alignment. Anger shows up as a result of the perceived discrepancy. One potential solution lies in simply naming what is angering both parties: Both people need to be able to say "this is what I want; this is what I see happening; and for me to be happy, this is what you and I need to do."

Now if your partner is committed to having a peaceful, loving relationship, then it seems to me they would be much happier giving you what you want if you just asked for it, instead of continuing to try and go in the back door using anger. However, if you consistently ask your partner directly for what you want and constantly get "No" for an answer, then I would ask you to ask yourself this important question: "What am I doing in a relationship with someone who doesn't care enough about me to give me what I ask for?" Or, you can continue to use anger in the hope that sometimes you will get what you want.

If you are a person who is often the receiver of someone else's anger, consider for a moment how everytime you acquiesce and give them what they want when they get angry, you are just reinforcing the behaviour of anger. Even though it may bring peace temporarily, you will be the recipient of their anger again down the road, as they have learned that is the way to get what they want. Again, clear, direct communication in regards to your boundaries is a stepping-stone toward the elimination of them continuing to use the grungie of anger. Remember, we don't control others, but we do control ourselves; and when we do something different, it will have an impact on those around us. If we do it consciously, the chances of it impacting in the direction we want goes up.

On a three-week road trip a couple of summer's ago with my family, I had the occasion to experience events that in one moment triggered joyful, warm feelings and then a short time later triggered a totally adverse reaction. For example, I would be really excited when we were standing on the edge of a cliff in the Grand Canyon and I could see the wonder in my children's eyes. Then moments later, we would be back in the motorhome and they would be making themselves snacks and leaving their plates and pop cans all over the small space we were calling home. The point for me was in recognizing that people often blame their mood for being the key factor in determining how they react to certain things. For example, I am in a good mood and so therefore I handle things better; on the other hand, I woke up on the wrong side of the bed, so look out world. Now, your mood may in fact have some impact on how you react to certain situations, but you have to ask yourself how many times you have been in a good mood and then something happens and you are instantly catapulted into being in a bad mood? This brings us back to the idea that it is more about my perception of the event that will dictate how I react, and my perception of the event has everything to do with my belief system.

MARTYR AS A GRUNGIE

Let's look at another example so you can really understand what I mean about how the payoffs and protections are the key to understanding ourselves better. This time, we'll look at the martyr grungie. For me, this has historically been my number one grungie. The Canadian Oxford Dictionary defines a martyr as "a person who is put to death for refusing to renounce a faith or belief; a person who suffers for adhering to a principle, cause; a person who suffers or pretends to suffer in order to obtain sympathy or pity." In this context, we will be talking about what is more commonly referred to as the "martyr syndrome."

This is a term that describes people who use self sacrifice and suffering as a way to attempt to control or manipulate their environment. It frequently includes being stuck in a victim mentality with resulting feelings of helplessness. So for me, it often shows up in the form of resentment towards the people I do the most for. For example, my youngest son has been drafted to the Western Hockey League and, when he turns 16, may leave home to go to another city to play at a more professional level of hockey than many kids ever get to. Part of what has gotten him to this level is his natural talent and his commitment to the sport of hockey. The other parts have a little something to do with his parents' willingness to drive him to practices, games, and all his extra training. In addition, we have invested thousands of dollars over the years on league fees and equipment.

Now sometimes when my schedule is very busy and his schedule is also very busy, and he isn't getting the kind of support from me that he would like, he becomes angry and short tempered with me and will criticize me for how much time I am spending at work. In these moments, he hits my martyr button and I feel wounded and victimized and reflect angrily back at him about how much I do for him. In addition, I point out how selfish he is since, if I didn't work as hard as I did, who would pay for all his training and equipment? I am sure all of you have a version of this scenario that you can relate to in your life. Some of you may even have compassion for me; others may wonder what I am whining about, since this is what I signed up for when I chose to have children.

The point I want to make is this: Just like in the anger examples above, you maybe learned the martyr grungie from someone else and it got embedded as a belief in your conscious or your subconscious, but you have maintained it as a behaviour because of the payoffs attached. In my case, my belief is not grounded in the I-must-sacrifice-myself-for-the-good-of-others mentality; in fact, it is more likely that my belief is that my worth and my value comes from doing things for others, and I will know I am contributing value when others tell me so. So I get poked when someone says I'm not doing enough—my subconscious hears that I am not valued and so feels wounded and victimized.

Let's connect this back to the concept of payoffs. So if you are a martyr, or you are in a relationship with a martyr, think about what the payoff for acting the martyr could be. What is the flash of pleasure that comes from stepping into "Oh woe is me"? It's possible, if not probable, that what you are looking for is simply the payoff of acknowledgment or recognition. So in my example, if Jesse understood how grungies and payoffs works, he would figure out that he would be more likely to get the support he needed from me by first acknowledging how much I do for him already and how he knows it must be a challenge for me to balance it all, but that what he really needs, despite how busy I am, is more support. Now, at 15, he is not quite that advanced and so, for me as the martyr, I have had to learn to speak truthfully and from my heart about how I feel when I hear someone saying I am not doing enough. In fact, I have been known to ask directly for that acknowledgment. For a martyr, this can be extremely humbling and is a direct step to moving out of the martyr grungie.

So for those of you out there who are martyrs, start asking directly for the acknowledgment you seek! And for those of you who have martyrs in your life and love how much they do for you, recognize them and they will be good for another 100,000 miles!

VICTIMIZATION AS A GRUNGIE

Let's look at another variation of the martyr, the grungie of victimization. The Canadian Oxford Dictionary defines a victim as: "a person who has come to feel helpless and passive in the face of misfortune or ill-treatment; a victim mentality." So essentially a victim is someone who has had something bad happen to them and believes that it is someone else's fault; or they blame themselves for being too ignorant to stop it from happening.

If we think about the evolution of victimization as a belief, it is not hard to see why many people feel like victims in certain situations, like car accidents. Turn on the television or open a newspaper, and you will find multitudes of advertisements for litigation lawyers who will help you punish the person or organization that has victimized you. And how many times has an adult said to a crying child, "Don't feel bad, it wasn't your fault; it was that terrible girl next door's fault," or some version of this. I'm sure there are many people reading this that can identify with this type of victimization, so it may be harder for people to see it as being a grungie. In fact, there are many people that feel quite righteous about the many experiences in which they have been vicitimized.

It is important to understand that the experience of victimization is very real; there are indeed many situations that have negative outcomes and that directly stem from the actions of others. The experience of victimization as a grungie, however, is when you let those experiences move you to a place of helplessness and powerlessness. It is when you stop taking risks because you have decided that there is no point in trying because someone or something will inevitably sabotage you. Or when you can't trust anyone because you are constantly anticipating betrayal, and then you bring about the betrayal you have been expecting simply because you wouldn't let anyone get close. You must get connected to the payoff or protections attached to the grungie of victimization to be able to begin the journey of changing it, consciously at first and then, over time, less than consciously (and more permanantly).

One significant payoff, then, is the excuse now afforded to you through the victimization grungie—the freedom to fail. So if you do take a risk and it doesn't work out, then you can simply say, "Don't hold me accountable for the outcome since I am the victim here, don't you know?" The flip of trying-and-failing is not even trying at all, saying, "Don't ask me to step up and play a bigger game because I don't have what it takes, and God knows it's not my fault."

Of course, on the protection side, it becomes easy to reinforce some old beliefs. The many years I worked in the shelter system showed me how strong the belief of perpetual victim can be and its resulting patterns. I saw many women come through the shelter, get tremendous support to get set up independent of their abuser, only to either return to the abuser and then come back to the shelter when violence struck again, or they would re-visit the shelter as a victim of a new abusive partner. In fact, after many years, I even began to see the children of clients coming into the shelter as the latest victim of family violence, repeating the patterns that their parents set. I am going to assume that despite the payoff side of victimization, most people would agree living life as a victim is a very heavy cross to bear, not only in terms of what it continues to attract, but also in relationship to the heaviness of the emotions that follow the powerless and wounded.

The solution for victimization lies in learning about the true power of accountability. In his book *Reframe Your Blame*, Jay Fiset defines accountability as: "a framing device that eliminates blame of self and others, providing the power of choice, participation, and co-creation of the experiences and results in our lives, real or imagined." Random House Dictionary defines it as: "the state of being accountable, liable, or answerable." Now you may notice that they are quite different definitions, and I would ask you to consider that Jay's definition has the power to transform your life and eliminate the grungie of victimization, if you apply it conceptually, and the Random House definition has the power to keep you stuck in endless cycles of blame and forever caught in the spin of victimization.

As previously mentioned, we live in a world that has deeply rooted patterns grounded in the cycle of blame. So for you to live a truly inspired life, you consistently need to live an accountable life, and for you to live a consistently accountable life, you need to eliminate blame on all fronts, both directed at your self and at others. Blame is the anchor that makes accountability impossible. As the Random House definition implies, by using words like "liable" and "answerable" your subconscious mind, based on all of its scripting, will inevitably translate that to mean "if I can't blame the person that did this to me, then I must be the one to blame." The constant message in this is that there is still blame in the mix. If blame is present, a wound is present; if a wound is present, negative energy is present; if negative energy is present, negative thinking is present; and if negative thinking is present, negative manifestations are guaranteed.

So let's look a bit closer at Jay's definition for some help not only with our understanding, but with the chance to shift the tides of change and start moving towards that more inspired life we have been talking about. The definition starts with the declaration that how we frame our experiences dictates how we feel about them. So, being accountable doesn't rely on certain external conditions to create a space for accountability; in fact, the conditions are always present because it relies on an internal mechanism.

For example, if I hit someone with my car, I can be accountable because that is an external reality and everyone agrees that it is conducive to owning up to my transgression; but if I get hit, then I am not accountable because I technically didn't do anything wrong. I was just in the wrong place at the wrong time. You can see that how you frame this external reality has everything to do with what comes next. Regardless of framing, what is true in both examples is that there was an accident. Framing is important not in terms of the reality of the situation, but the reaction that follows. So, in Jay's definition, I start by acknowledging that the truth of accountability is as a way to frame all experiences; I know it is how I frame my experiences that has the most impact. Then it takes you to the place of recognizing the importance of no blame.

Furthermore, Jay's definition, unlike the Random House definition, also clearly states that there is no blame of self or others. From there, it challenges you to recognize that not only do you have power, but you have a choice, and by nature of the fact that the event occurred to you in your life, you have participated in it on some level. Jay's definition ends with a clear statement that

Chapter Three: GRUNGIES AND PAYOFFS

35

this participation applies regardless of the external reality and challenges you to recognize that much of what is perceived as reality is imagined.

So the accountable version of my car accident example would be: I choose to be in my car in this moment, and perhaps I co-created this experience as a result of my desire to get a new car. In fact, I have been saying for a while now that it would be nice to get a new car, and now perhaps I will. Or maybe I allowed myself to be distracted from the task at hand because I was thinking about the chaos of my day, and I was driving below the speed limit, and this is a good reminder that I should leave the office at the office. There are any number of other possibilities depending on your willingness to look for the lesson in why this event occurred to you at this moment in time and space.

HOW MY IMAGINATION IMPACTS MY REALITY

The impact of imagination is primarily explained scientifically by looking at a concept called "memory reconsolidation." Memory reconsolidation is the process of previously consolidated memories being recalled and actively consolidated. It is a distinct process that serves to maintain, strengthen and modify memories that are already stored in the long-term memory. Once memories undergo the process of consolidation and become part of long-term memory, they are thought of as stable. However, the retrieval of a memory trace can cause another phase that then requires an active process to make the memory stable after retrieval is complete. It is believed that post-retrieval stabilization is different and distinct from consolidation, despite its overlap in function (ie. storage) and its mechanisms (ie. protein synthesis).

So without overwhelming you with the "scientific" understanding of brain function, we will suffice it to mean that when we revisit memories that were originally encoded within a short period time of the event occurring, it is possible that we rewrite some of our recall of the event simply based on what was triggered inside of our belief system. It is the rewrite that becomes encoded and therefore we remember it as stable and are absolutely convinced we are remembering correctly, yet somehow someone else may have experienced the exact same event and may honestly remember it differently.

So what is an "original memory"? The process of interpretation occurs at the very formation of memory, thus introducing distortion from the very beginning. Rarely do we tell a story or recount events without a purpose. Every act of telling and retelling is tailored to a particular listener; we would not expect someone to listen to every detail of our morning commute, so we edit out all the extraneous material. The act of telling a story adds another layer of distortion, which in turn affects the underlying memory of the event. This is why a fish story, which grows with each retelling, can eventually lead the teller to believe his own fishy tale.

Several studies have been conducted on human memory and on subjects' propensity to erroneously remember events and details that did not occur. Elizabeth Loftus performed experiments in the mid-70s demonstrating the effect of not just an individual's belief or perceptions of an event via the beliefs systems filter, but also addressed how a third party can introduce false facts into memory. Subjects were shown a slide of a car at an intersection with either a yield sign or a stop sign. Experimenters then asked the participants a few questions, falsely introducing the term "stop sign" into the question instead of referring to the yield sign that participants had actually seen. Similarly, experimenters falsely substituted the term "yield sign" in questions directed to participants who had actually seen the stop sign slide. The results indicated that subjects remembered seeing the false image. In the initial part of the experiment, subjects also viewed a slide showing a car accident. Some subjects were later asked how fast the cars were traveling when they "hit" each other; others were asked how fast the cars were traveling when they "smashed" into each other. Those subjects questioned using the word "smashed" were more likely to report having seen broken glass in the original slide. In this way, the introduction of false cues altered participants' memories.

Courts, lawyers and police officers are now aware of the ability of third parties to introduce false memories to witnesses. For this reason, lawyers closely question witnesses regarding the accuracy of their memories and about any possible "assistance" from others in the formation of their present memories. However, psychologists have long recognized that gap filling and reliance on assumptions are necessary to function in our society. For example, if we did not assume that the mail will be delivered or that the supermarkets will continue to stock bread, we would behave quite differently than we do. We are constantly filling in the gaps in our recollection and interpreting things we hear. For instance, while on the subway we might hear garbled words like "next," "transfer" and "train." Building on our assumptions and knowledge, we may put together the actual statement: "Next stop 53rd Street, transfer available to the C train." Indeed, we may even remember having heard the full statement.

Experiments conducted by Barbara Tversky and Elizabeth Marsh corroborate the vulnerability of human memory to bias. In one group of studies, participants were given the "Roommate Story," a description of incidents involving his or her two fictitious roommates. The incidents were categorized as annoying, neutral or socially "cool." Later, participants were asked to neutrally recount the incidents with one roommate, to write a letter of recommendation for one roommate's application to a fraternity or sorority, or to write a letter to the office of student housing requesting the removal of one of the roommates. When later asked to recount the original story, participants who had written biased letters recalled more of the annoying or "cool" incidents associated with their letters. They also included more elaborations consistent with their bias. These participants made judgments based upon the annoying or social events they discussed in their letters. Neutral participants made few elaborations, and they also made fewer errors in their retelling, such as attributing events to the wrong roommate. The study also showed that participants writing biased letters recalled more biased information for the character they wrote about, whereas the other roommate was viewed neutrally.

Memory is affected by retelling, and we rarely tell a story in a neutral fashion. By tailoring our stories to our listeners, our bias distorts the very formation of memory—even without the introduction of misinformation by a third party. So the final statement inside of Jay's definition is as vital and important to living an accountable life as is the parts around no blame and owning your power inside of each event.

HOW CAN I SHIFT THE CYCLE OF VICTIMIZATION?

So in order to truly eliminate the payoff of victimization in your life, you must ask yourself this question whenever recalling a victimization experience: "Is every part of this memory true?" If the answer is yes, then ask yourself the question: "How do I feel by choosing to believe the memory is true?" And then the next question is: "What would happen if I choose instead to look for a gift or a lesson inside of this experience that I co-created with the person or people involved, and perhaps even with God, which is intended to help me grow?" I might realize that nothing in my life is a coincidence. I know how I contributed to the event and am willing to learn the lesson to begin to shift the tide of my thinking to promote a new way of thinking and therefore a new way of attracting.

Let's look at this from the perspective of some of my clients from the shelter. Imagine if a battered woman could sit back from the horror of her experience and begin to identify that she had chosen this relationship in the first place. She must realize that she does have power, and that for her to exercise that power, she must recognize that something in her belief system is reinforcing her inability to leave her abuser. These beliefs might be something like, "I don't deserve to have someone cherish me," or maybe "men have the right to control their women," or "I won't get anything better," and so on.

So instead of wasting all of her precious energy in attempting to convince her partner to change, she must see that this event has showed up in her life as an opportunity. Perhaps it is an opportunity to break the pattern of abuse and to change her beliefs about herself and therefore begin the process of manifesting and attracting a new style of relationship that is more consistent with her new frame of reference. The lessons she could take from this would be, "I have tremendous strength; it has required significant power to stay alive in this situation, and what I now know to be true is that I will need to call on that same power and strength to help me in the transition to a violence-free lifestyle."

Unfortunately, the way we often address the issue of family violence is that we collectively deal with it the same way we deal with many similar situations; we say, "it is not your fault; he is 100 percent responsible for being violent, and of course it's hard for you because he has taken away your self-esteem. Without self-esteem, it will be very hard for you to break free. You will need a lot of external support from us to make sure you can stay free of him. In fact, you will likely have to go back to the shelter at least six times before you are ready to make a final break." With that framing, is it any wonder that clients re-visit shelters over and over again?

I HAVE THE ABILITY TO CHANGE

So in summary, we choose the negative emotions of grungies because somewhere along the way we acted out from our grungies and we got some sort of payoff or pleasure from acting and feeling that way. When confronted with a particular type of event external to us, we are triggered inside of our belief system and our response is consistent with the belief that has been triggered and our recall of what we get when we act in response. If nothing changes and we don't consciously engage pattern interrupts, we will go on indefinitely making choices that don't seem to have the payoff that they did originally, but that we are now stuck with in a cycle of repeating patterns. To end this cycle, we must first tell ourselves the truth of what the grungie is, what the payoff is and what is a more powerful way to meet the need long term and consistently.

If we have not addressed your number-one grungie in our examples, then I encourage you to pick from the list, sit with your pen and paper and honestly write out how acting and feeling this way works for you. Then look for the belief that has been created in conjunction with the grungie, ask yourself about your memory recall of the events that caused this belief to become what it is, and then consider a re-write that includes accountability using Jay's definition. If you can do this for each one, your ability to act cleanly and powerfully, versus negatively and disempowered, ruled by your conscious and less-than-conscious beliefs, goes up exponentially.

Seeing as external victimization and procrastination are two common and significant grungies that many people carry and suffer inside of, we will devote the next two chapters to dealing with these directly.

Chapter Four:
DEALING WITH TYRANTS

TYRANT OR MISPERCEPTION?

As mentioned in the previous chapter, we understand that victimization experiences can occur, but we also discovered that no one or anything can hurt you unless you allow it. When you feel victimized, you often become hyper-focused on the other person, your perceived perpetrator. You spend time contemplating how you can somehow exact your revenge on them, carefully pondering how you can hurt them, or at the very least get them to see how badly they have hurt you and hope they wallow in guilt and remorse.

Most people see the common-sense truth that no one has the power to hurt you emotionally, spiritually or mentally, and you really are not powerful enough to hurt anyone, other than physically perhaps; but yet somehow, those who have been victimized can't help but run through the many victimization events in their heads and remember how hurt and sad they were, or likely still are. Even though it doesn't make any sense, it sure feels like others have the power to hurt you. Perpetrators of victimization also can't help but get a small flash of pleasure when they think they have been able to cause someone else's suffering.

So in an ideal world, we would stay anchored to the idea that others can't hurt us and we can't hurt others and work towards simply being accountable for our own choices and keep our focus where we truly have control. However, considering we don't live in an ideal world, I believe it is important we learn to recognize how we allow others to tyrant us, and how we attempt to tyrant others. To do this, I will be referring to Carlos Castaneda's book, *The Fire From Within,* in which he enumerates the various types of tyrants. Let's start by understanding and defining the top-five types of tyrants, not to mention two other tyrants that are self-wrought:

1. The first type of tyrant is **the irritator**. The irritator is the type of person who does annoying things or has a habit of just getting under your skin. Irritators are not really hugely significant in the larger scheme of things, but they can catch you off guard and can command your time, energy, attention and resources.

2. The second type of tyrant is **the manipulator**. Manipulators are people who are cunning, clever and devious, and, as we discovered in the previous chapters, are usually angry or martyrs. They scheme and attempt to trick you into doing things you might otherwise not do, often without your conscious awareness. They will say or do whatever it takes to get you to do what they want. If they are quite adept at manipulation, manipulators can bypass your critical thinking because they have identified some inner weakness or Achilles heel that you hold inside.

3. The third type of tyrant is **the tormentor**. Tormentors are those people who are caught in their own pain and suffering and will take that pain out on others. They try to bring others to their level of suffering, since misery loves company. They may torment you with words and can go as deep as to abuse you emotionally and physically, as reflected in our examples of women in shelters who are attempting to flee this type of tyrant. Tormentors target whatever they believe will upset or control you the most. Their intent is to reduce the spark of happiness and joy from your life.

4. The fourth type of tyrant is **the melancholic**. Melancholics simply oppress you with their sadness. They are energy drainers and are often deeply attached to their "sob story." They work

primarily with pity, and not only do they drain you, but they may cause you to become negative in reaction to them. Melancholics can accurately be thought of as an extension of the grungie of victimization, when actually being victimized turns into the victim then becoming a perpetrator.

5. The final type of external tyrant is **the dictator**. They are major tyrants and in fact seek to control and dominate your will and your energy. Dictators are able to use any of the aforementioned methods to get what they want.

HOW WE TYRANT OURSELVES

There are two other types of tyrants that are not external to us. They are the ways in which we tyrant ourselves either through self-pity or self-importance. When you have self-pity, you avoid being accountable for your life, whereas self-importance causes you to become attached to how others perceive you.

You must understand that the ability to tyrant you does not lie solely in the hands of the person who is tyranting you—it lies in the reality of you allowing yourself to be tyranted. To stop the process, you must learn how to deal with the tyrants in your life. Because you allow tyrants into your life, the gift is knowing you can disallow them as well.

At this juncture, you should stop reading and make a list of the tyrants in your life and recognize how you allow them to have tyrannical power over you. You must name your tyrants before you can deal with them.

HOW BEING A WARRIOR CAN HELP ME

Now the truth is that to break free of this cycle, you must begin to step into the strength of warriorship, and I'm not talking about the warriorship that requires you to meet people on the low road and engage in battle. More precisely, I'm talking about warriorship in terms of exercising your Will, having a capacity to practice Self Control, using Discipline, Forbearance and mastery over Timing. In Carlos Castaneda's book, *The Fire From Within,* he explains each of these five traits in more detail. Let's look at each of them more closely:

Will

Engaging the power of your will, simply put, is setting yourself a clear intent. In Chapter Two on Intention, we learned to understand the power of our conscious and less-than-conscious intentions. Leveraging your will also means consciously setting your intention.

Self Control

Some of the types of tyrants in your life will try to exploit your inability to maintain internal self-control. Essentially, this means that you are giving away your power. Taking that power back is the key to maintaining your inner authority and neutralizing the tyrant. This would be where you would exercise the programme of "Stop, Look, Choose." To do this, you must work on staying grounded, holding your center and not allowing yourself to be caught off balance. You must stop your automatic ways of reacting, look at the various perceptions and possible truths and then consciously choose how to react.

Discipline

Tyrants will attempt to create rewards and punishments designed to control your behaviour, and in this way they try to exert discipline over you just like they would over a child. Self-discipline, on the other hand, is training yourself to look at the plethora of choices you have and to choose those that are more likely to get your more of what you want instead of more of what you don't want. To achieve self-discipline, you need to be well connected to your intuition. You must set your goals and then make clear decisions about how best to move towards them. Discipline also means not becoming a tyrant yourself by learning to assert yourself productively versus becoming aggressive in reaction to others choices.

Forbearance

Forbearance allows for the possibility of responding to a tyrant in your life by choosing no response at all. In essence, when you feel the pressure tactic being sent your way, you choose not to respond or react and don't allow it to influence your actions. Forbearance is the capacity to not move into resistance, to practice surrender in the moment and to leave a space for consciously choosing.

Timing

Timing refers to choosing the best moment to respond. There is a bit of intuitive magic to having good timing with a tyrant—it is a combination of holding a strong and clear intention, committing to the specific action you wish to take, and consciously, but patiently, looking for the best moment to take that action. Having good timing also includes having the willingness to make the jump when it comes time to act.

DEALING WITH YOUR TYRANTS

When it comes to the ways in which you deal with your tyrants, all of the above attributes have value but the most important one is, by far, will. Your will is that ability to create and sustain an unwavering intent and the capacity to take deliberate and sustained action to make that intent manifest, no matter what the inner dialogue and limiting beliefs that show up to get in your way. To exert your will is to harness your life force. It allows you to be accountable and humble all at the same time.

All of the remedies presented here may take some courage, but trust lessons will emerge regardless of your level of perceived success in pushing back against your tyrant. This success in turn leaves room for the power-based experience of growing and learning from every experience that shows up in our lives, even those experiences that we perceive as challenging and negative. You have called the tyrant into your life to help you grow, so you can either stagnate, stay stuck and play small, or you can embrace the opportunity to meet your tyrants head on, learn the lessons and move on. The more you embrace the attributes of the warrior, the less likely you will continue to manifest and allow tyrants into your world.

Previously, I asked you to make a list of all of the tyrants in your life and to list how you allow them to tyrant you. Now, I want you to look at the attributes listed and decide which one or ones you will engage to begin the balancing work of taking your power back and how it will show up directly in your interactions with the tyrants in your life.

Chapter Five:
PROCRASTINATION

Procrastination is something we all do to some degree; but the real question is, how much does it have to hurt before you are willing to do something about it? Research on human motivation—trying to figure out what drives people to do the things they do—suggests that any actions resulting in negative reinforcement discourage repetition. So how do we explain procrastination? For many of us, procrastination is such a significant part of our lifestyle that we forget that a major source of our emotional discomfort comes from this habit.

Webster's Dictionary defines procrastination as, "To put off doing something, especially out of habitual carelessness or laziness." "Careless" and "lazy" are two emotionally charged words that can reinforce debilitating self talk and feed your need for procrastination. If procrastination is an issue for you, it is important that you address the cause and the degree to which procrastination is impacting your life.

You would be considered a "light" procrastinator if you only occasionally put off doing something. Examples of this are deciding that you should do the laundry, but then finding a television program that appears more exciting and the laundry gets neglected, perhaps not even until after the program is over but until the next day. The negative impact of this, however, is minimal. "Heavy" procrastinators are people who consistently put off all tasks and challenges, often indefinitely. It matters little to them whether the task is big or small; whatever the magnitude, "I'll do it later" is the motto, but later never comes. The impact on your life in this case is more severe.

The degree to which your life is impacted by your procrastination will be relative to whether you consider yourself a "light" or a "heavy" procrastinator. Regardless of which type you are, in order to effectively reduce procrastination you must first address what is the primary motivator behind your choice, just like we did with grungies in Chapter Three. Some of you may resist the idea that procrastination is a choice, and even less that it is a grungie, because admitting that you have a choice in the matter would imply that you have some power to change your result.

In fact, you may feel so debilitated by your procrastination that you are convinced there must be something inherently wrong with you and, therefore, is outside of choice. The prefrontal cortex is the part of the brain that science has discovered to be physiologically tied to the act of procrastination. This area of the brain impacts brain functions such as planning, impulse control and attention, and it acts as a filter by reducing distracting stimuli from other brain regions. If there is damage or low level activity in this area, an individual's ability to filter out distracting stimuli can be hindered, ultimately resulting in poorer organization, a loss of attention and increased procrastination.

This is similar to the prefrontal lobe's role in Attention-Deficit Hyperactivity Disorder (ADHD), where underactivation is common, and many individuals who deal with ADHD are often found to be tremendous procrastinators. But is it, in fact, procrastination or could it be that they have just forgotten what they were going to do and so it mimicked the choice-driven part of procrastination? My oldest son has been diagnosed with ADHD, and I could never send him to do more than one thing at a time since he would always come back empty handed. He also procrastinates and I see them as very different considerations.

However, if you choose to accept that physiology is the only reason that procrastination exists, then your solution will likely lie in choosing medication and dealing with its side effects; or maybe enlisting with a therapist whose job it will be to reinforce your dysfunction by telling you, "it's not your fault; it's a physiological issue, so you must just learn to live with it."

I would like to propose an alternate solution, regardless of your physiology, that will put the power back into your life: ALL procrastination is a choice. No physiological excuses will be supported here. As I mentioned earlier, it is my presumption that all behaviour manifestations start with a root thought or a deep-seated belief. They may eventually evolve into a physiological manifestation, but if you ever hope to change your physiology, you must first change your thoughts. And to change your thoughts, you must become more accountable for your current frame of reference.

WHY YOU PROCRASTINATE

If you have previously reflected upon this question and are already aware of your map of reality, meaning the thought process that feeds your propensity to procrastinate, then you could move right to the suggested solutions. However, if your self awareness is limited or blocked, I am going to propose four potential reasons why most people procrastinate:

1. Because Something is Difficult
When you decide that you lack the skill or expertise to do some-thing, your self talk convinces you to not even attempt it. You might choose to do something easier instead, or you might not do anything at all. While conducting interviews with my co-workers at Personal Best, I heard statements like, "I am pretty sure I have almost always decided I won't do something good enough, so I don't even bother starting," or "I'm pretty sure I have a core nega-tive belief about myself that is deeply rooted in perfectionism. This stops me from taking risks and results in procrastination."

2. Because Something is Time Consuming
When you feel that a particular task is time consuming or will take up a considerable block of time, you try to avoid ever starting it. You convince yourself that you must do something else that is quicker. Some of my personal interviews resulted in statements like, "Leaving things to the last minute impacts the quality of everything I do, so I decide I have no time and then waste an

inordinate amount of time and energy worrying about what I am procrastinating doing."

3. Because You Are Afraid

In this case, you procrastinate because you are afraid of failure in a particular task and you don't want everyone to know that you failed or to blame you for failing. You keep postponing the task and avoid ever doing it. When interviewing my co-workers about their experiences with procrastination, one woman indicated that she felt her most consistent experience of procrastination was intimately linked to her already acknowledged fear of failure and that this fear had effectively eliminated her passion to envision or to dream about what was possible, knowing that she would never do it.

4. Because Something Else Appears More Satisfying

This type of procrastinator views their responsibilities negatively and avoids them by directing their energy into other tasks. It is common, for example, for relaxed-acting, procrastinating children to abandon their schoolwork but not their social lives. This type of procrastination is a form of denial. The procrastinator avoids situations that might cause them displeasure, indulging instead in more enjoyable activities. In Freudian terms, these procrastinators refuse to renounce the pleasure principle and sacrifice the reality principle instead. They might not appear to be worried about their work and deadlines, but this is simply an evasion. Personal interviews affirmed this with statements like, "I get to avoid the things I don't really like to do. It is a form of escapism."

SOLUTIONS

You may see a part of yourself in one or more of the above examples. Regardless of which one, or perhaps how many of them are true for you—you may even have a different motivator or reason—there is a solution. It begins with, once again, being accountable and acknowledging that your are choosing not to do something. From there, you must decide consciously what is motivating you to choose not to do the task. Once you are clear about what motivates you, you can re-frame your thought process with a new frame that empowers and motivates you to get it done!

NLP (Neuro Lingusitic Programming) has a very fast technique for changing beliefs. It's based on the observation that whenever a belief changes, there's a transition from state to state that looks something like this:

1. Conviction

2. Doubt

3. Disbelief

4. Open to a New Belief

5. Uncertainty

6. New Conviction

The assumption is that those states can be anchored just like anything else.

To deal with each state, the NLP technique involves six corresponding "stations." When you're first starting this, you should write out all six stations on pieces of paper and arrange them in a circle around you for added visual effect. The stations are:

1. Current Belief

2. Open to Doubt

3. Museum of Old Beliefs

4. New Belief

5. Open to Believing

6. Sacred Place

When you're doing the imagining, make sure you try to feel the total experience—visual, auditory, and kinesthetic (feelings). Try placing the paper markers at different places in your home and moving around between them; physically moving has value in regard to changing anchors.

1. Stand at station 1 (Current Belief)—Think about your current belief and about how it feels. Examples could be: "I don't have enough time," or "I don't have the skills necessary," or "I am afraid," or "I am lazy."

2. Move to station 2 (Open to Doubt)—Think about something that you consciously and knowingly doubt, and how that feels. An example could be that you knowingly doubt you are going to get the promotion that is available at work. Now think about your target belief and how it feels to doubt that it may be true. Other examples could be times when you aren't afraid, or times when you have risen to a challenge despite a skill deficiency and have actually got it done.

3. Move to station 3 (Museum of Old Beliefs)—Think about a belief that you used to have but no longer have, and how that feels. An example could be that you never thought that you had what it took to run a marathon, but in fact you just accomplished it last month. Now think about your target belief and how it feels to no longer believe it. As you leave station 3, imagine that you're leaving that belief behind in the museum.

4. Move to station 4 (New Belief)—Think about the new belief you want to have.

5. Move to station 5 (Open to Believing)—Think about something you don't believe but are open to believing, and how that feels. Now think of your new target belief and how it feels to be open to it.

6. Move to station 6 (Sacred Place)—Think about one of your strongest and most sacred beliefs, and how that feels. Now think about your target belief and how it feels to believe it with the same conviction.

Once you feel anchored to the new possibility, kick yourself into gear and take action! The more you try to push past your procrastination, the more motivated you will be to not CHOOSE procrastination ever again!

Chapter Six:
THE POWER OF ANCHORS

Imagine having the power to do a very simple act and instantly be able to change your mood, your emotions or even your energy level, and perhaps even eliminate grungies and procrastination from your life forever. Sounds exciting, doesn't it? With this power, you could even influence other people without them being consciously aware of it. What I am about to tell you is easily the most powerful technique you'll ever learn to help you change your emotions and the feelings of other people around you.

This method is being used by practitioners of NLP and is intended to be used with integrity and clean intention. I share it with you to help you live a more inspired life, but also to help you to support others as well.

First, let me present a scenario to you.

Let's say you are watching a sad movie. While totally engrossed in one of the most dramatic scenes, you barely notice the sad background music that is being played. A few weeks later, you hear the same sad song on the radio. In a brief moment, you're immediately shifted back to the experience. You suddenly remember that particular dramatic scene, the actors who tore your heart out, and even the friends you went to the movie with. You feel the same sad sensation all over again. You recollect the sentimental mood because of that same music.

That sad music is called *an anchor*.

What is an anchor? An anchor is a compelling and influential connection of something seen, heard, touched, smelled or tasted with a specific memory or representation. You associate an emotion experienced in the past with a state correlating to the present.

HOW TO USE AN ANCHOR

Let's say you want to experience happiness.

Go into a quiet room. Reflect on a time when you had a very happy experience. It can be when you heard a joke that was so funny that it brought tears to your eyes. Or it can be another experience when you ran out of breath because you were laughing too much.

Now focus on reliving that funny experience. Engage yourself thoroughly on re-experiencing that fantastic feeling. Picture the joker's funny face, hear their humorous antics, taste the food you were eating at the time, smell the odour, and try to remember everything else that was going on around you as you were laughing your heart out.

Then create an anchor for yourself. You could lightly slap your face, shake your hands in exhilaration, squeeze your thumb and middle finger together or twirl your head; just do anything you can think of as long as it's something that creates an intensity within you. After about a minute or two, let go of the anchor while still remaining engrossed in that state. Wait for a few seconds before breaking out of that state.

Now, next time you are feeling sad or want to feel happier, engage the anchor you created. For example, if the anchor you created was a twirl of your head, you will conceptually need only twirl your head and a feeling of happiness will emerge.

You can use any of the anchors on the following page depending on your situation and preference. You may even invent one or two of your own.

1. Clench your fists.

2. Stroke your hair, chin, nose, or eyebrow.

3. Press two fingers together.

4. Whistle a tune.

5. Rub your hands.

6. Shake your legs.

7. Shout a lively word, such as "power," strength," or "energy!"

8. Pat yourself on the back.

9. Hold a piece of jewelry that you always wear tightly in your hand.

In case you're still a little tied up, here's another case.

Let's say you want to finish a very important project, but you're too tired and bored of doing it. Here's how you can conquer your negative emotions.

Go to a quiet room. Recall a time when you feel so passionate or enthusiastic about a certain endeavour. It could be a time when you persistently studied hard to ace the Board Exams. It could be a time when you were assigned an exciting project that you did with so much energy and commitment. Remember to relive the emotions you've felt with intensity. Really feel it.

Then create an anchor using any one of the anchors listed above. You can create one of your own that you think will be most effective. Be imaginative.

After around a minute or two, let go of the anchor while still remaining engrossed in that state. Wait for a few seconds before breaking out of that state. Remember, the more intense or concentrated the emotions are while you're recalling the experience and employing the anchor, the better the outcome.

HOW TO USE ANCHORS TO HELP OTHER PEOPLE

Let's say you want to help a co-worker with confidence. Wait for a time when they have just done something really awesome and amazing. Give him/her an awesome gift honouring what a great job s/he did, compliment him/her in front of your other co-workers, or do anything you can think of that will really get him/her connected to that feeling of pride.

Then rub his/her shoulders when s/he's so happy, confident and listening to you speak. When a time comes when s/he is struggling, rub his/her shoulders. His/her confident feelings will return, and you can feel proud of your part in helping someone along.

You may succeed the first time you apply an anchor, or you may not. Some people succeed during the second, fifth, or even the 20th time. The important thing to do is practice. Don't give up if the first few attempts fail. With sheer determination, you can do it and remember to do this for the good of all concerned. It is a subtle yet very effective way to continue to override the conscious mind.

Chapter Seven:
TRUST AND FORGIVENESS

TRUST

There are multiple definitions out there to explain what trust is, but the one below is quite consistent with many of them. The Canadian Oxford Dictionary defines trust as, "faith or confidence in the loyalty, veracity, reliability, strength, etc. of a person or thing."

Essentially, when we say that we trust someone, we are really just saying that we trust that they will act in a particular way and that way is in alignment with our values and what we believe are behaviours that constitute honesty, integrity and reliability. If those attitudes or behaviours are present in another person, we will usually say that we trust them.

When trust is broken, however, it is then usually because of a breach or a stepping outside of who someone said they were or what they said they believed in, or when they act out of alignment with our belief system or definition of what those traits afore-mentioned mean to us.

Now, in an ideal world, when you first meet someone, it would be prudent and helpful for you to have already determined in your own mind what your standard of trust is. A lot of heartache could potentially be avoided if people were able to predetermine that their standard of trust differs too much from someone else's and therefore a clash of beliefs and a breakdown in trust is almost always assured. So, if we can identify our trust boundaries early in the game, we may choose to never play together at all.

For example, for me to trust someone, I need to believe that they value a win-win relationship and that they will always look at both sides of a coin. I need to know that they will look for ways to ensure that we are both okay no matter what our engagement or interaction is centered around. If we are looking at doing business together, I want to know that they are not only looking out for themselves, but that they believe my success is important to them as well. If we are involved personally, I want to know that when we meet a challenge or a difference in opinion and have to make a decision about what to do next, they will not only consider what they need, but will also be attentive to what I need and find creative solutions that work for both of us.

For me to trust someone, I need to know they believe in what it means to be held personally accountable. This means that no matter what is happening in their life or inside of our relation-ship, if we are struggling, I need to know they will not just look to blame me or somebody other than themselves, but that in fact they will always be willing to take a step out of the situation and become the observer; that they will look at what their part was in how the situation arose and will be open to creative brain-storming as to what the lesson is and how to grow inside of those life lessons. If they have this concept working in their lives, I know that we will able to navigate through virtually anything, and therefore I fully trust them and the relationship.

I also try to gauge how authentic people are. Authenticity, to me, means how they are in relationship compared to what they say they believe. If someone's words and actions are out of alignment, I may not totally trust them. I am more trepidatious around them and tend to watch them more closely. I will then often have them tested as to how much incongruence is present. Sometimes testing takes the form of asking them direct questions like, "I observed this, you said that, can you explain to me how that happened?" If they are willing to own up to their deception and speak to what motivated them, I will trust them more than if they lied on top of a lie. I believe that we are all image makers to some degree, shapeshifting and trying to fit in, pretending to act in a certain way so we get approval. How "fake" someone is determines more of how much I trust or don't trust them.

I also have various degrees of trust: Some people in my life I trust with my life; some people I trust them to borrow my car or no more than 20 dollars; some people I trust will disappoint me. It all comes down to the same thing—for me to trust you, you will need to fit my definition of what constitutes a trustworthy person.

My experience of many of the people I work with is that they walk through life saying "I don't trust people," and when they are asked to define what "trust" means to them, they aren't able to articulate it clearly. So then, when challenged with the question, "How can you say you don't trust someone if you can't even define what the word 'trust' means to you?" they usually answer with some version of a story or recall of an event with a past "someone" in their life . So, based on "who" that person was or what that person had done, they basically decided that anyone who resembles that person is likely going to do the same thing to them in the end. For many people, this decision begins to set generalized standards that are often rooted inside of traits like gender (all men cheat; all woman are manipulative), wealth (rich people are dishonest and selfish) or age (teenagers are dangerous and self absorbed).

So what you need to understand is that I am not suggesting those generalizations are correct or not correct, but what I do want you to understand is that if you carry those ideas and have anchored to them, two things are happening in your life. Firstly, based on how law of attraction works—what I focus on expands, what I resist persists—you will be actively calling those types of people and relationships into your life. This doesn't mean that those types of people don't exist, but it just means as long as you focus on believing what you believe, the Universe will continue to send those people to you as a way of making you think you're right. We so desire to be right, even if it hurts! Secondly, when people who don't fit your stereotype appear, they don't really have a chance with you as you will test them over and over again. If they are like most people, at some point they will just get sick and tired of all the testing and will just abandon you, thus "proving" you right.

Now, with that idea in mind, and despite everything we have just learned regarding trust, consider the following sentence: I can trust somebody, but in a completely negative sense. Along these lines, I can trust that you will betray me, I can trust that you will lie to me, I can trust that you will be late, and many other versions of how that might look. We could call this the "shadow" side of trust.

So overall, what is very important when it comes to understanding trust is that whether your standard of trust is centered around particular ways of someone being or doing, on the "light" or the "shadow" side, you must know what constitutes your personal standard of trust. For your relationships to hold the remotest possibility of success, you must find a way to articulate your standard of trust to the people who are in relationships with you so that they are better able to make clear decisions about how they will live up to your stated standards. You may also want to look at whether or not your standard of trust is reasonable, or if maybe, because of past experiences, you have become jaded and it is keeping you from developing any kind of openness to the possibility of a different type of relationship than your past relationships.

Unfortunately, having stated standards are not always a guarantee that success in your relationship is assured. If you were to poll the average adult, I am sure you find that well over 90 percent of people would say that their trust has been broken at least once. As Oscar Wilde said, "Trust is rarely pure and never simple." When we speak of trust, knowing and speaking our standard is helpful, but what also becomes important is that we acknowledge that inside of each of us, there exists a light side and a shadow side to our trust. Knowing this and embracing it can be a direct path to forgiveness and to trusting other people more (which is the foundation of any relationship), but most importantly, it could also be the direct path to self forgiveness and to trusting yourself more. If you trust yourself more than anyone or anything else, it becomes much easier to be decisive, to take risks and, in the end, to shift when things go sideways.

Lets explore the concept of the shadow a bit more to help you understand what I am saying.

Embracing The Truth of our Shadow

The shadow is the part of us that we're ashamed of, the part we don't want people to know about. It's the part of us that we hide away in the closet of our minds and our actions. The shadow is dark; it's secretive, primitive and shrouded in mythology. And if we ignore the shadow, it tends to say, "Well, I'm going to embarrass you then. I want you to notice me and, in your unwillingness to name me or own that I exist, I will take control and show up at the most inopportune time possible."

I remember once when my youngest son brought home his report card and had received a failing grade in his Drama class. Now, to help put this into perspective, my youngest son is an academic and an athlete. At the time of writing this book, he is 15 years old. He does well in school (for the most part) and even better in hockey, where he has been drafted to play in the Western Hockey League. So to say he has been pretty successful in his young life would be an accurate statement just simply based on results.

But back to the report card: When I first saw his failing grade, I instantly challenged him and expressed how surprised I was, knowing what he was capable of. His response to me was quite matter-of-fact; he felt that Drama class was an insignificant part of his life in the grand scheme of things, and he felt that the public school system could do a better job at offering a broader variety of choices to fill the gaps in between reading, writing and arithmetic, and based on his lack of interest in Drama, he consciously chose not to apply himself.

Now, instead of being open to allowing his perspective and point of view—he is only 14, after all, so what does he know about anything?—my shadow side stepped into the space and out of my mouth came some version of, "Well, that's just great if you are okay with being a failure; if you're content with being mediocre, then that's fine." My light side would have said, "I appreciate your perspective and point of view—on some level, I agree with you—and in truth, what I want for you is to 'hold the space' that even in the presence of something you don't really like, since life puts us in those situations quite often, you could still be successful and know what it is like to be successful in all situations. To learn how to create success when it doesn't come easily is a powerful lesson and can have leverage to transfer to other areas of life."

Now you might say that this sounds like something lots of people would say, and I'm sure you can think of many times when you said something that you wished afterwards could have come out differently. It's not that I carry a tremendous amount of guilt or shame, but it is abundantly clear that my shadow side has had a non-supportive impact on my relationship with my youngest son and proves that no matter how much I value acting and speaking from my light side, my shadow side exists. It was this same part of me that caused me to have an affair during my relationship with the father of my children. So whether my shadow side has caused relatively small damage or more significant damage to my relationships, if unchecked it could have the potential to wreak havoc in my life. As long as I keep it under control, my shadow side allows me to honour my humanity and creates a series of experience from which I can learn about myself and grow as a person. Because of this self-awareness and acknowledgement of my shadow I then also have an opportunity to trust myself more, to be more transparent and honest with others in my life, allowing for a development of trust in the relationship despite the fact I may mess things up sometimes.

So when you exhibit so-called light and shadow qualities and behaviours, you are not flawed; in fact, you are complete. When you are comfortable with your shadow and can meet and embrace your shadow, accepting that this is how the Divine wisdom made you, then you become attractive beyond measure and your life is an adventure. You are authentic when you are comfortable with your ambiguity, and nothing is more beautiful than authenticity. When you are comfortable with your body and your strengths and weaknesses, you radiate simple, unaffected humanity. Trust will inevitably follow.

Let's take this another step and explore a concept that will help you embrace others in a deeper way, help you accept yourself in a more powerful way and in the end potentially increase your ability to be trusting on all levels.

The whole of Creation is a contrast, in tension, a Divine discontent. We live in a world of universal truths and one of those fundamental truths is the Law of Polarity. The Law of Polarity states that everything in the universe has an opposite. There would be no inside to a room without an outside. If you referred to this side of the page as the front, then the other side would be the back. You have a right and left side to your body. Every up has a down and every down has an up. The Law of Polarity not only states that everything has an opposite, but every opposite is also equal. If it is three feet from the floor up to the table, it is three feet from the table down to the floor. If it is 350 kilometers from Edmonton to Calgary then it must be 350 kilometers from Calgary to Edmonton; it cannot be any other way.

If something you considered "bad" happened to you, then given the Law of Polarity, there has to be something "good" about it. If it was only a "little bad," then when you mentally work around to the other side, you will find it will only be a "little good." If there were only lightness and joy than how could you know it as that, you would have nothing to contrast it with and so would not then know it as light and joyful.

To find your shadow, you have to be dedicated to a journey of honest reflection and to begin the journey toward risking rejection and disapproval. Think of this journey as going back to retrieve parts of your life that have been abandoned because you felt too ashamed or guilty about them. The anger that erupts from the shadow is attached to past events that were never resolved. Even though those events are over and gone, their emotional residue remains and is often having an impact on your results right now. One of the things I love about being a hypnotherapist is a significant part of inner healing work is about searching for the shadow and working with it to move towards healing, acceptance and integration. And in our willingness to own, heal and integrate our shadow, others in our life can trust us more as we move closer to authenticity.

To make matters more difficult, shame, guilt, and fear cannot be accessed by thinking. The shadow isn't a region of thoughts and words. Even when you have a flash of memory and recall such emotions, you are using a part of the higher brain—the cortex—that cannot touch the shadow. The journey of descent can only begin when you find the doorway to the lower brain, where experience is sorted out not according to logic, but according to emotion.

No matter how free you feel from shadow energies, they exist inside you. If they didn't, you would be in a state of total freedom, joy and unboundedness—the type of energy that a child lives inside of. Children are not born with the instant capacity to feel guilt or shame, but when they are first confronted with feedback that a choice they made was bad or "wrong," the shadow is born. I have meet some pretty happy and content people in my life, but I'm not sure I have meet anyone that could say they were in total freedom, joy or unboundedness. The people that come the closest are usually people who have done years and years of personal development work and have learned to identify and embrace their natural knowing in regard to what works and what doesn't. They are able to make choices based on their beliefs and not scripted ones that belong to others. They can acknowledge when their shadow side is present, honour why they chose from that space and feel free to make a new choice.

Shadow energies make themselves known whenever a controlled situation turns unexpectedly anxious or causes unforeseen anger or dread. If you feel guilty or ashamed of yourself after you experience these emotions, then you have touched, however briefly, on the shadow. Remember the example of my encounter with my youngest son's report card: Did I feel some guilt and shame; absolutely. Did I wish in the next moment that I could take it all back; totally. Did I take a withdrawal from our trust and love account; I sure did. Did I learn something about my belief system and did I feel grateful for that learning; definitely.

An eruption of irrational feeling isn't the same as releasing it—venting is not purification, so don't mistake an outburst for catharsis. When your shadow energy truly leaves, there is no resistance anymore, and you will finally see something you didn't see before. In fact when you reach this type of surrender, you are able to acknowledge your part in how any situation has manifested into your experience.

Rage can be tamed by breaking up the shadow side of your personality into more manageable bits. When you have been treated unjustly or feel personally harmed or victimized, the natural emotion is anger. If this anger can't get out, it festers and grows in your shadow side. Lashing out when holding it back no longer works; this type of anger leads to a cycle of rage. When rage is present, trust is likely absent.

This rage can put you in a kind of double bind: If you lash out and return the harm done to you, you have done something that is not acceptable by most people's standards; but if you keep the anger inside and harbour it, you will be doing something equally detrimental, though only to yourself.

Yet rage, as I mentioned above, can be tamed by breaking it down into manageable bits. By being transparent and authentic about how we feel and what we are choosing to do based on those feelings, we can process the smaller bits one piece at a time. Negative emotions that feed off certain aspects of the shadow become very manageable when we are willing to name them and work with them instead of against them.

The shadow is dark. Everyone has a shadow as we understand the natural contrast between darkness and the light.

The shadow is the root of all of our secrets. We store impulses and feelings that we wish to keep private. We withhold truths about our experiences and our choices.

The shadow is dangerous. Repressed feelings have the power to convince us that they can kill us or drive us to the edge of insanity.

The shadow is shrouded in myth. For centuries, people have seen it as the lair of dragons and monsters. In our modern world, some would refer to it as our ego.

The shadow is irrational. Its impulses fight against reason. They are explosive and totally willful. It drives us to the edge of acting from the reptilian part of our brain.

The shadow is primitive. Most people would deny that it even exists, and almost all are resistant to looking at it.

Negativity receives its overwhelming power from the fact that it feeds off all these qualities at once; a secret, dark, primitive, irrational, dangerous, mythical evil is much less convincing if you break it down into one quality at a time. But this process of bringing darkness down to scale won't be convincing until you apply it to yourself. But your ability to apply it to yourself can only occur when you accept the reality that your dark side exists, and you must also see the value in stepping into authenticity.

It is then, and only then, that we can begin to foster more trusting relationships with all of those we are in relationship with.

FORGIVENESS

If we can accept the idea of the light side and the shadow side, and we can accept that the Law of Polarity exists, then perhaps we can open ourselves up to the possibility that when trust is broken, it can be healed and therefore can be regained or earned. In these circumstances, it will be the concept of forgiveness that provides the bridge back to trust.

Let me preface this portion with the idea that if you were truly able to embrace the concept of accountability, then forgiveness would not even be on the table. When living inside of accountability, we understand that all things are perfect by design, and all events—whether perceived as positive or negative—are co-created with our participation in order to support us in our soul's growth and evolution. Therefore people who come into our lives, especially those that we perceive to have caused us harm, are in fact here to support us and are as deserving of our respect as those that we consider to have helped us in a positive way on our evolutionary journey. If we embrace this idea of accountability, then conceptually there will never be anything to forgive.

But considering that most of us have not evolved our ego selves enough to have absolute accountability, how to forgive becomes a topic worthy of conversation. For the purposes of understanding, let's work with an example that many of us can relate to either in the form of direct experience or of knowing someone who has faced this issue. As I mentioned earlier, as I was working towards evolution with my shadow side fully engaged, I made the less-than-conscious choice to engage in an extramarital affair. What started out as a reaction to my unhappiness ended in me stepping righteously outside of what my values and my belief system would normally dictate, in an unhealthy and unhelpful way. Unfortunately, my marriage did not survive, but I have since worked with many couples where the relationship has been able to recover. In these cases, a significant amount of healing and forgiveness has to be present when someone has had an affair.

Relationships that are broken by infidelity can lead to permanent damage or even divorce. But those who are willing to repair and rebuild the relationship can do so with persistence and effort. In the beginning, both parties must exchange forgiveness. This means that both people have to admit that they have some accountability for the breakdown of the relationship. Often, one person will carry more of the challenge than the other person, especially where an affair is concerned. But perhaps the other spouse had developed a cold attitude toward the offender, driving him or her to an outsider for affection. Even if there appears to be no direct connection between the two parties' behaviours and the affair, a breach like this provides the opportunity for self-reflection and a commitment to improved relational qualities, such as better communication and patience. From here, new agreements must be formed and a commitment to working through the ego challenges and the trust considerations will require support and sometimes objective mentorship from an outside source. I have sat with many couples as they worked through the anger and sadness that comes from being involved in an affair.

Essentially, there are some core fundamental ideas that you must engage to fully move toward forgiveness. Here are some of the typical steps that many couples follow when working through a relational breach and can apply in many situations that may benefit from forgiveness:

1. The first core concept is the concept of **understanding**. Stephen Covey, in his book *Seven Habits of Highly Effective People*, speaks of the habit of "seek first to understand and then be understood." Without understanding the nature and ways of our common humanity, forgiveness has no soil in which to grow. If I acknowledge my own shadow, then does it not seem reasonable to acknowledge that others have a shadow side that they must meet as well?

2. The second core concept is the concept of **freedom**. Without accountability, freedom is an illusion and forgiveness becomes an empty act. Our true power and true opportunity to evolve comes inside of our willingness to learn life's lessons and to grow through the application of these lessons. When we understand and apply the lessons, then and only then can we become free of all those feelings and ways of being that kept us small and stuck.

3. The third core concept is the concept of **remedy**. Without remedy and rebalance brought by forgiveness, how can life ever be cleansed from the repetitive re-enactment of yesterday's wounds? If we never learn from our past mistakes, then we are destined to recreate the patterns of our past. What we resist persists and what we focus on expands. If we can forgive ourselves and others, then and only then will the focus shift and our ability to manifest more of what we want and less of what we don't want becomes possible.

4. The fourth core concept is the concept of **warmth**. Without trial and error, we would not learn, and the warmth of forgiveness makes way for us to try again. In Neale Donald Walsh's children's book *The Little Soul and The Sun*, children and adults learn that everyone who comes into your life is an angel that, at a soul level, has agreed to lower their vibration and bring us harm to remind us of who we really are.

5. The fifth core concept is the concept of **enhancement**. Forgiveness teaches us to stand against the wrongful act or offence, not the human life that has committed it, or else we deny someone else's future opportunities. This creates a space for all of us to mature and evolve and feel safe enough to disclose our shadows and know that, given guidance and understanding, others will hold the space that our transgressions are not who we are, but rather are reflections of our behaviours and are often the mirrors and sparks for change.

6. The sixth core concept is the concept of **hope**. We each have in us the ability to hold the best of another in trust in the sanctuary of ourselves. By forgiving someone else, we leave the contextual space that others may be able to forgive us when we step out of our light.

7. The seventh core concept or idea is the concept of **continuance**. The exercise of forgiveness is the longing for the establishment of what ought to be, and the love of this as an inner devotion is connected to the love of life continuing. If we are not evolving, we are dying, and what we desire most is to live, fully and completely. Not willing to forgive serves no one, and mostly it prevents your own personal growth and evolution.

When these core concepts are embraced, understood and applied, forgiveness is possible. Now I want you to make a list of all the people who you feel you would benefit from forgiving. Give yourself the gift of writing and walking yourself through each of these seven core conceptual steps in regard to each of those relationships. When you feel some success inside of this, give yourself the gift of a few days and then bring that person to mind and notice how you feel. If you really want to test your level of forgiveness and they are accessible, you should call them or meet them for a coffee and again observe how you feel. Most of all, notice post-forgiveness what has changed in your inner world and subsequently your outer world.

Chapter Eight:
GOAL REALIZATION

Just about every human being at one time or another has asked himself or herself the question: " What on Earth am I here for?" And most humans will have asked themselves this question long before they ask the question: "How can I then live my life from a more inspired space?"

This universal question of "what is my purpose?" has baffled humanity since time began, and it is even more debated today because we live a more complex, fast-paced and constantly changing life—everybody seems to be in a hurry, racing against time. But despite our busy schedule, this question keeps lingering on, especially when we have time to stop, recollect and are trying to find our inner self.

Some people might be able to give you an answer, while others may have an answer but are quite doubtful that they have the right one, and still many of us have unanswered questions. Whatever specific reason each of us have for justifying our existence, there is one universal reason: "To find happiness and to live life from a space of inspiration versus obligation." We owe this to ourselves.

Now we have spoken at length in this book about how our sub-conscious impacts our ability to set clear intentions, but this chapter will be devoted to working with the conscious mind. Please bear in mind that for any of this therapy to work, you will need to have previously done the work of clearing and healing the parts of the mind that will keep you from manifesting the life you desire.

Happiness and inspiration come in many forms, and each is unique from the other. Happiness and inspiration means embracing the Divine Providence in your life—it is having found your true love and raising a family. It is a life of legacy, power or wealth. It is good health. It is in serving others and countless more. Some of us may be happy for just one reason, but often it is a combination of several.

Despite the way that we perceive happiness to be or whether we truly desire inspiration, goal setting (also called "visioning") and realization of said goal is a vital part of achieving happiness. Great opportunities abound in life—it is entirely up to us to hold onto these opportunities and align them with our goal. I cannot overemphasize the importance of goal realization in pursuit of happiness and inspiration. Realizing a goal creates a feeling of fulfillment. Either way, we can choose to be one of these three types of people: a goal achiever, a failure or an in-between. Again, what you are is entirely up to you.

Personally, I think we stand to gain a lot if we choose to be an achiever—in thinking this way, we stand a good chance of being one—and in most cases, this gain will most likely exceed our expectations or imagination. Speaking of imagination, imagine a person whose life is aimlessly drifting without a purpose. You might say "what a waste." Such is a life being spent without setting and attaining goals. Now think of a person that you know who has reached the ultimate goal in his/her life. Wouldn't you want to know his/her pathways to success? Wouldn't you want to follow in his/her footsteps? Of course you do. We all do. We all want to succeed in life, and the way to do it is to set goals and attain them. Vision makes getting up in the morning so much easier.

For most of us, though, setting and attaining goals seem to be a far-fetched, difficult task. We sometimes think that it is a task reserved only for the intellectually gifted, for the lucky few or for the affluent. How can I create a vision when it takes everything I have to just get through my day?

Indeed, it can be a difficult task, especially considering what we know about how our belief system impacts our results. But to say that it is reserved only for the gifted, lucky or affluent is inaccurate. This is an excuse to fool ourselves and once again fall into illusion. Often, because of our belief system, we are not being mindful of our own potentials. We just keep on drifting life away like a horse with blinders on. We keep on concentrating on our daily routines and activities and life's short-lived pleasures that we tend to forget about, set aside or even ignore our goals in life.

However, this kind of lifestyle not only has something to do with our belief system, but it also has something to do with our attitude, and this is the attitude we need to change. We have to adopt a goal-oriented attitude. We have to get out of our comfort zone and venture into that jungle out there by leading an active life that will bring happiness not only to ourselves but to others as well. As we learned earlier, we are all apprehensive of change, but this is one change for the better and it will be worth a hundred, maybe a thousand, fold over.

NOW IS THE BEST TIME

There is no better time to focus our attention to visioning and goal realization than right now. Frankly speaking, yesterday was a better time. In fact, the day before yesterday was even better than yesterday. But the past is the past—there's no point in griping over time spent. However, to delay any further would be an indication that you have missed some of the work on grungies or you are still stuck in the spin of your old belief system.

I can't overstate the importance of time when it comes to goal attainment. Each day, week, or month's delay may mean lost opportunities, and this might derail the time-frame that you set for yourself to attain your goal. Remember Chapter Five on Procrastination: We know that what we do with our time cannot only get in the way of achieving our goals, but it can also have significant impact on how "inspired" we feel.

I could easily use the example and experience of writing this book. When I decided I would write it, I got busy and took a writing course, I hired a book coach and couldn't wait to start writing. I had a year contract with my book coach, which, at the time, seemed like more than enough time to write a best-seller! Well, as life and subsequent time constraints took hold (as I so often allow it to do), the book was being written at a snail's pace, and every time I sat down to write, it would take me so long to get started because I had to go back and reread what I wrote last since so much time had elapsed in between my writing sessions. The more times I had this experience, the more frustrated I became and my inspiration to sit and write was less and less. In fact, when the year was coming up and my book contract was about to expire, I had only written three chapters! I extended my contract for three more months, and at the date of this writing, I have extended it for an additional three months, making my one year process—which, remember, felt like plenty of time—into an eighteen-month marathon and not always the "joyful" experience I had been anticipating.

Though there is usually no specific or particular "due date" for goal attainment, we must not treat goal attainment half-heartedly. Give it concentrated attention, effort and energy, and the rewards will come to you in more ways than you expected. There may be instances in which delays are unavoidable, but be sure to give it a think-over and exhaust all possibilities to minimize each delay. If delays are still unavoidable, then you must patiently give way to it, but under no circumstances should procrastination take its place in your pursuit. In my book writing example, I enjoyed spending days engaged in the process of writing my book while I was sitting on a beach in Mexico, miles away from the chaos of my life and the mountains of snow and winter blues at home. I made the choice, and many heard me say, that I wasn't coming home until this book was done. If I had stuck to my guns, though, I'd probably still be in Mexico.

Like any other endeavour, it is human nature to delay. Nobody's perfect. But every time it does, we must pick up a lesson or two from each experience. As the saying goes: "Charge it to experience." If you notice you are repeating certain patterns, or if the things you want never seem to get to you, you are likely dealing with some block in your subconscious. Despite my time consideration, I know one of the other things that was getting in the way of me finishing my book was my confidence in writing a book that people would actually want to read. On some level, this has been a conscious belief, but one that based on results that I have had some difficulty in overcoming.

Speaking of experience, this reminds me of the importance of history lessons. There is another old adage: "Learn from the mistakes of others; you can't live long enough to make them all yourself." This is one of the reasons why we have history subjects in school. You may wonder how history is related to goal realization. I also used to wonder why we had to study history lessons, thinking about what good it would do for the present and future generations. I used to think that we can't turn back the hands of time to correct mistakes, so studying history is a waste of time and energy.

But then I realized that, through history, we can learn from the achievements and failures of other people. We can imitate and analyze the traits and characters of great achievers and at the same time avoid the pitfalls of failures committed in olden times. History gives us an insight from which we can draw countless lessons that will greatly help us to make better decisions on certain aspects of life, particularly those related to goal realization.

In fact, one of my favourite authors and gurus, Gregg Braden, in his book *Fractal Time*, wrote about how history is our greatest teacher, both practically and spiritually, since evidence suggests that history has a tendency to repeat itself; so if we can understand the timing of certain events, we can anticipate what is coming next and change something enough that we could impact the possibility that events in the past, which had devastating results, do not have be repeated. It gives us leverage and power to impact our present and change our future.

We all know that time is money. Therefore, spending time to pursue our goal is time well invested. Even if, after spending lots of time on goal attainment without ever achieving it, we can become history ourselves. We can pass our experiences (be they good or not so good) onto the next generation so that they can serve as lessons for them. In effect, this will save time for our successors who wish to continue our pursuit.

One way or the other, we can say to ourselves that we have contributed or done our part, no matter how menial it is, as long as it is intended whole-heartedly to reaching our goals or manifesting what we dream of.

GOALS KNOW NO BORDERLINES

At one time or another, we've come across articles that touch on issues like racial, age or gender discrimination, leading to a suppression of values or convictions. You cannot let those issues affect your pursuit of goal realizations. Your target goal does not look at your colour or race. You may be black or white, yellow, brown, red, or any combination thereof. You should not be discouraged just because you're not so young any more, or you are a woman, or you're a man without the "right" education.

In short, goal realization has no limitations according to race, age, sex, convictions, religion, economic prosperity, educational attainment, experience, fame and influence in society—you name it. The only thing that might limit your goal-realization potential is the on-going battle between your conscious intent and your less-than-conscious intent. We have spent some time already trying to help you identify why your conscious and less-than-conscious intent may not line up, but let's spend some time now trying to help you figure out how to bring them into congruence using your conscious mind. This in no way takes away from the importance of doing the work to uncover what your personal grungies or evaluating why you procrastinate; this will just help to fill in the space that's left when you clean up the unconscious parts of your mind.

IT ALL STARTS WITH A DREAM OR A VISION

We all know what dreams are all about. Some dreams are shady images of what seems to be part of what's really happening in our life. These types of dreams mostly occur while we're asleep; in hypnotherapy, we call it "dream venting." On the other hand, the "dreams" that I'm referring to here are more so dreams about what we want from life, or what we want to happen to us, or what we want to be in the future. Most boys between age three and six would respond to the question "What do you want to be when you grow up?" with answers like: "I want to be a pilot," or "I want to be an astronaut" or "I want to be just like Superman!" Girls of about the same age would probably respond to the same question with: "I want to be a doctor" or "I want to be a teacher."

These answers show the gestation of young boys and girls dreams about what they want to be when they grow up, even if some of the answers may be too exaggerated. However, these are all answers that are as realistic today as they will be when the children grow up to be adults, and if they stick to pursuing their wants or desires, even the Superman goal—with a few modifications—could still come into reality.

Did you notice though that every time these future-oriented questions are raised to young children, the answer always starts with "I want to be..."? Wanting to be somebody special or to do something important is the start of creative or desired dreaming. Wanting works hand-in-hand with dreaming and starts to evolve toward the goals we intend to set and attain. Wanting something badly can be so powerful that we start enacting plans to make things happen the way we want them to. The drive to succeed gets even more powerful when the desired outcome will produce good deeds for the benefit of many. Somehow, an altruistic spark is ignited that starts to kindle and glow in the dark, letting the desire take its shape and molding it into something beneficial and worthwhile.

Now fast-forward and ask an adult what their sacred dream or desire is; it is not likely to be prefaced with "I want" but more so with: "Well, right now I'm doing…" or "What I would like to be doing is…." So you have to ask yourself: What impact does being focused on doing have on our dreaming or visioning?

Even though the dreams that occur while we are asleep are different from our dreams of the future, there is nonetheless some degree of interrelation between the two. When we persistently concentrate on our wants and desires, those wants and desires sometimes manifest themselves in our sleep dreams and give us a vivid vision of how we can make our ambition turn into reality. So much so that when we wake up, we have fully developed a direction or plan on how to execute our ambition even when it previously seemed so vague or far-fetched. Or if we consciously plant the seeds of what we desire when we are just falling asleep or when we are just waking up (the alpha brain-wave pattern), we are in effect planting seeds in the unconscious mind that, given good conscious sunshine and nutrients, can grow into making our dreams a reality.

But even if our dreams are vague or seem impossible, we must keep them alive in our minds. By keeping them constantly on our minds, we are continually injecting fuel that keeps the fire of our dreams aflame. What used to be a vague vision of our dreams will slowly but gradually turn vivid as we commit it to memory. After a time, what used to seem impossible starts to look possible.

And when we have reached this stage of possibility, we cannot resist the urge that overtakes us to mold it into a reality. We can't wait to start turning the wheels of development. The sheer force of this urge will propel these wheels to move, no matter how small the movements are, because so long as it moves, we want to see how it develops. We love to see progress. We want to see improvements. Then, without even noticing, the moves may start to pick up speed. And just to think: This all started simply as dreams in our minds.

Creative dreaming is a burning desire that keeps our ambitions going, and by holding on to it, you will turn it into a reality. There is no stopping goal realization as long as there is creative dreaming. In fact, some schools of thought would say that the word want is disempowering to the law of attraction because, even after we get what we want, we are left in a state of wanting. But if we can use creative dreaming as the tool to inspiration, then we can powerfully replace the concept of "wanting" with a reflection and affirmation grounded in the precept: "I am so happy and grateful now that (my chosen sacred dream) has now manifested into my life."

ACT ON IT

A dream is a vision in our mind. Creative dreaming without action is no way to goal realization.

Typical examples of acting on your creative dreams are the Great Wonders of the World, the magnificent landmarks that symbolize the greatness of a nation: the Statue of Liberty in the United States, the Big Ben in England, the Taj Mahal in India, the Great Wall of China, the Great Pyramids in Egypt, and numerous more. Imagine if these great ideas, these creative dreams, were not acted upon; would we ever have had these great wonders to be enjoyed by people from every nation on Earth? What kind of achievements would each nation have to show if their great thinkers just sat on their grand ideas and never acted on them?

You'd probably say: "Oh well...at least we still have the natural wonders like Niagara Falls, Mt. Fuji and the beautiful coral reefs." Yes, but these are God's creations. God did not create us in His/Her own image if S/He thinks we won't be using our creativity and put it into action. S/He might as well take it away from us. S/He expects us to act on it.

So what's keeping us from acting on our ideas, other than procrastination of course? We know that this inactivity has something to do with our belief system, consciously and less than consciously, but let's name a few of the reasons that are often part of the collective consciousness that feeds many belief systems. Fear of rejection is often one of our biggest deterrents, and our need for approval is another major one. There's also the fear of failure, fear of sinking into a deeper depressed state than we presently are, fear of totally losing all we've got if we don't succeed and fear of taking risks.

These fears are all perfectly legitimate, but nonetheless we all have to take risks at one time or another. Risks may present themselves to us for a variety of reasons, big or small. There are risks we can do without, but there are also risks that leave us no option but to take charge and act on it. Risks come in many different forms. For comparison purposes, let us consider two risks: winning or losing when we gamble, or taking chances in pursuit of a goal.

The risks involved in gambling are for non-thinkers. This is tantamount to "luck" risk, not "good judgment" risk. Risk of this kind has no room in goal realization. It is like ignoring safety rules on the road just for kicks; it's a come-what–may attitude—short-lived and done to satisfy a craving.

However, risk in pursuit of a goal has a definite, lasting purpose, a purpose that will bring untold benefits once you've achieved your goals. It is a risk worth taking and is for thinkers, not for happy-go-lucky non-thinkers. Risk in pursuit of a goal will bring stability and security to your life, and ultimately leads to happiness.

Whenever fear grips you, think positively. Look at it this way: Will you ever get anywhere if you don't take risks to act on your dreams? Will you ever be satisfied with your inaction, five, 10, or 20 years from now? If you notice, there is one common denominator that is holding us back from acting on our dreams: that thing called "fear." Fear is the biggest stumbling block to acting on a creative dream and it practically holds everything to a standstill. So it is imperative that we eliminate fear from our feelings to clear the way to our goal.

To overcome this fear, we have to face fear directly. This confrontation requires courage, and it is important that you understand that people who have courage do not forego the experience of fear. The difference between someone with courage and someone immobilized by fear is that the person who has courage felt the fear but did it anyway.

Let us take a typical example: Say you have a fear of public speaking. In fact, studies put this fear as either the number-one fear for most people or, in other cases, it is second only to the fear of dying. So the worst-case scenario is that you will get tongue-tied and spoil your entire speech in spite of having committed the entire speech to memory. You become the laughing stock of the audience. But put these thoughts aside and don't let them prevent you from speaking in public the next time around, because if you do, fear will have won and you will be cowering from this public-speaking fear for the rest of your life. To win over your fears, draw lessons from your failures and capitalize on them the next time around. Don't stop until you have successfully given a good speech. Once you do, you will have actually turned the tables around—this time, it will be fear that fears you, and you will become a person who has courage!

Here's is another example with a somewhat different twist: Say you are a lifeguard and you just failed to save a drowning person who was perfectly saveable. Now this is a big failure because a life was lost, but in spite of this horrible accident, you shouldn't give up being a lifeguard just because of one mistake. Instead, think about the other lives you have saved before and will be saving if you continue to be a lifeguard. What if next time you were able to save a person who was in an otherwise hopeless situation? Wouldn't this off-set or overcome your previous failure?

The idea here is to always give your best, regardless of the results. When you give your best, it doesn't get any better because it is already your best effort.

When you act on your dreams, think of your actions in a positive way. What you think is what will happen. What the mind can conceive, the body can achieve. Believe that the outcome of any action depends mostly on how we set our mind to it. Remember that our actions originate from our thoughts, and the ultimate result is dictated by our mind as well. If we think it will fail, it will; whereas if we think it will succeed, it will. Mental attitude is the master of the actions we undertake.

When your mental attitude is set a certain wayfor a longer period of time, the more difficult it is to change to an opposite mindset. If your mind is set on negative thoughts, the more difficult it will be to change to positive thoughts if you do not act on it immediately. However, if your mind is already set on positive thoughts for a long time, it will remain firm in this attitude as time goes by. This is the power of consistency.

Many a time, I have had a client tell me, "I tried your suggestion and used my affirmations every day for two weeks and nothing has changed. These affirmations don't work." The truth is that affirmations do work, but perhaps the belief they were rewriting was so deep that they needed to do the affirmations for up to six months for it to penetrate down to the required level. Defeat is imminent if your thoughts are in this direction and you give up too quickly. You may say "I told you so" when an action you expected to fail has failed just to satisfy yourself, when in fact you are really looking for an excuse or taking the easy way out. The end result is still a failure, and this puts you at the mercy of your old belief system once again.

On the other hand, success is imminent when your thoughts say you will succeed. Even if you fail the first time, you will learn from your failure and you will have the information needed to address the less-than-conscious contradiction. When you try again, you will ultimately succeed because you keep gaining more experience. Keep on trying and persevering! You should never let up, and when success is at hand, you will have defeated defeat.

Also consider how achieving success will impact you personally in terms of keeping a positive attitude and having your conscious mind and unconscious mind supporting you in successfully achieving your goals. Then consider the impact it could have on your family. With this positive attitude, every member of your family will experience this blessing and it will grow stronger in time.

Therefore, every member will carry this positive attitude and role modeling with them for the rest of their lives, ultimately resulting in a successful and happy life. And, unknowingly, you are also bonding the family closer together for a longer lasting relationship.

The same thing is true outside of your household. We are all familiar with the phrases "Show me your friends, and I'll tell you the kind of person you are" and "Birds of a feather, flock together." We are who we keep as company. We are what we think we are. A person, in time, can shift totally from one personality to another, especially if that person is the type that follows a leader. If you have leadership qualities, you are, in effect, the one who persuades the follower to change to your kind of attitude. The stronger personality has the stronger attitude to persuade. It is a good thing if the leader is the optimistic type, since all followers will follow suit. The other way around usually leads to disaster.

So if you have children, make sure they are in good company. And you can do so by making yourself into an example.

CONDITIONING THE MIND

The shortest distance between two points is a straight line. In goal achievement, the first point is our dream, the second point is our goal and the distance between them is the action we take to turn the dream into reality. A straight line may mean zero obstacles or troubles, but in reality, this likelihood is next to impossible to achieve when we understand the power of our subconscious—but that doesn't mean it's not possible. However, we must always be prepared for any possibility and must try to keep our road to goal realization as trouble-free as possible.

When we set ourselves to achieving a goal, we need to fashion our conscious mind to be attuned to it. We have to align our thoughts in the direction of that goal. We need to get to our goal via the easiest manner in the shortest possible time. In other words, we have to condition our minds.

Let us differentiate between different attitudes, especially those attributed to the way we direct our thoughts to goal achievement. It may sound contradictory at times that two characteristics are almost exact opposites, yet we still want them both practiced. For example, sometimes some of us may quip: "I must not delay things, but I need to be patient enough to wait".

Consider an elderly woman who went to a cardiologist for a check-up. The doctor prescribed some medicines to keep her blood pressure within controllable limits plus gave her recommendations on certain types of food she has to avoid. After a couple of weeks, when there wasn't much improvement in her condition, she went back to the same doctor who, this time, referred her to another doctor where she was diagnosed with a slight kidney problem, which was the reason for her frequently changing blood pressure. So she was again prescribed some medicines and was again told another list of foods she mustn't eat. But she soon found that some portions of the two food recommendations contradicted each other, and she wound up with a very strict limited diet, making her miss out on some vitally needed nutrients. Dismayed, she ignored part of the recommendations, used practical sense and methods and took moderate amount of various nutritious foods. In the end, it turned out better for her. Please be mindful that ignoring a doctor's orders is not recommended, but it does suggest that being a good consumer and occasionally getting more than one opinion can be helpful. Learning to trust how your body speaks to you is also important.

By practicing practicality in regards to the mental characteristics that we need to adapt, we must lean on the positive and aggressive side of the action we have decided to take to achieve our goal. We need to persevere and be persistent no matter what. However, learn to stop and rest for a while if need be and continue again after regaining your strength. We can stop temporarily but not permanently. We must have a burning desire or passion to attain our goal but must not burn ourselves out. Don't let stress and tension affect you and your health. We must act on ideas immediately but must be patient enough to wait for results without unnecessary delays on our part. Some processes just take time.

Not everything can be done with shortcuts. We must work on the goals that we like and are familiar with, yet we must not stop to learn more about it, especially those pertaining to new innovations and technologies. Be positive, practical and aggressive in the pursuit of your goals.

There is no substitute to a peaceful mind. To be able to think straight and in a clear manner, a peaceful mind is essential. It is like a clutter-free household; we come home relaxed even after a hectic day.

Take a mind full of tense feelings and negative emotions: Where do you think this will lead to in goal realization? Rather, this will lead to goal disintegration. You have to remove all the garbage (i.e. negative impressions) from your mind to give way to clear, tense-free positive thinking.

Success, failure, good times, hard times; they all happen. They are a part of life. But when failures and hard times occur, sometimes we become so affected by these circumstances that we become slaves to them. We feel so bad that we become affected by them in almost everything we do. We lose control, and then trouble drops in. And all these value judgments, if we analyze them, are based on the way our minds respond to them, usually in a negative way.

To counteract the hard times, we need to think about the good times, but to do this, we need to capitalize on how the situation turned from "good" to "hard" by drawing lessons from it. The positive answers will eventually pop out of our minds, and we will begin to feel good because we now know the answer to "correct" this failure the next time around. And the next time around, it should be acted upon immediately, thereby blanketing hard times with good times in a short period of time.

Let your mind control the situation in a positive manner. Do not let the situation control your mind. In fact, if you are having a hard time with this, take the next few days and, as you are getting ready for sleep, make the last thing you think about what you are grateful for from your day. Notice your vibration or energy in the morning when you awake and notice what energy you are able to hold through your day to support you in your goal acquisition, both short term and long term.

When we set to pursue a goal, we must consider goals that can be achieved in a manner wherein we have more of a hand in controlling the processes. Remember we only control three things— how we think, how we feel and how we act—but we do have influence over many others and the degree of influence we have is directly proportional to how well we manage and control these three things.

What we discussed way back in Chapter One is how to control a situation that has already happened by being mindful of how we react to it. All events are neutral; we attach signficance to the events, and the signficance we attach dictates how we feel, and how we feel determines how we act. Now, we must consider how to control a situation that we think may happen, sort of like pre-empting what we think will happen. These two concepts may seem similar enough, although there is a difference between the two.

This type of situation control tells us to concentrate on goals that we can heavily influence, so we can direct the outcome to the way we plan it. You may think this is manipulative, but let me explain why it isn't.

For example, let's say you want to get into the business of making ready-to-cook French fries. If you are going to buy potatoes from a farmer who dictates the price in the market, you're bound to have problems beyond your control. One of the solutions to continue in this business would be to look for more suppliers, preferably those that see the value in establishing a win-win relationship; or better still, you must be prepared to plant your own potatoes. These ways, you will have a ready solution to a potential problem.

Get involved in goals in which you have control of your own resources or work with others that you feel like you have influence with. In short, choose goals that are familiar, comfortable and you have more experience in.

As another example, let's say that you want to be a life coach or mentor. A coach or mentor must be both a good listener and a good adviser. If you are good at listening to other people's problems but cannot give sound feedback except reactions like: "Oh, that's too bad...that's awful...that's terrible," you cannot be a coach or mentor. Consequently, if you're a good adviser but a bad listener, you cannot be a coach or mentor either. Come to think of it, how can a person give sound advice if s/he doesn't listen well? Maybe instead of coaching, go into sales where good conversationalists are needed.

As a part of everyday living and in the course of setting and realizing our goals, we are usually faced with different kinds of adversity that hinder our growth and our development. Such troubles may directly affect the goal that we are aiming for, others are more indirect, and still others have nothing to do with our goals except that they take up some of our time and make us feel bad. Either way, adversity slows us down, making us feel as if we want to give up.

From these troubles, we can either become cowards or a stronger, wiser person, learning from them. It all depends on how we handle adversity. These would be the typical times during which we default to our grungies like victimization or martyrdom, but remember that these are no longer parts of who you are—they are just reflections of your belief system, and so you do have the power to change them.

For example, when I first made the decision to become a steward of the Personal Best courses, I took many risks. I gave up a secure job, moved miles away from my friends and family and ventured into the unknown world of capitalism. Having been in the non-profit sector my entire adult life, I was wary of the capitalist world as I held many scripted beliefs about its evils. Over time, however, I began to discover that my values were not in jeopardy, and I actually enjoyed the experience of what felt like a true win-win situation. I brought something of value to my clients, and in their willingness to pay for that value, I could grow and extend my reach even further.

Now in 2009, I was given the opportunity to extend that reach even further than I ever imagined was possible. I was offered the chance to steward the entire province of Alberta, and despite much internal resistance, I took the leap and expanded my business in a significant way. It didn't take long for me to discover that during the time that my business was expanding, the rest of the world was contracting due to the recession, and the resources I needed to just keep my head afloat was not happening. I experienced moments of feeling completely defeated and overwhelmed with the amount of responsibility I was carrying, and I felt helpless to impact my situation in a positive way. I manifested shingles, brought stress to my family relationships and had frequent headaches. I had days where I thought it would just be so much easier to get a job where someone else had to deal with all the risk and I had a guaranteed income.

But the whole time I was thinking those negative thoughts, I kept reminding myself that I had never done the work at Personal Best for the personal gain or the financial security—I did it because of the passion I held for the process and the way it impacted people. So instead of running from my goal realization, I looked at what choices I had made that had perhaps brought me to this place of near-personal and professional collapse and took those insights and re-visioned a new dream. I chose to "fail forward" and am happy to say that I am rebuilding the scaled-down version of the part of the company I am steward for and have become a better person, a better business owner and a better coach for all those I come in contact with. Some of those awarenesses I came to on my own and some came with the support of my coach, my friends and others invested in my success, including my connection to my faith and the divine.

To be on the winning side, we can draw support and advice from our family and friends. But the best support that we can get is from the power of faith, which you will read about in Chapter Nine. Ask Spirit to come to your aid, but do so with intense depth and sincerity. Spirit will clear your mind to find a solution to your trouble. Spirit works in wondrous ways, and that is why we must keep our minds clear—so that it may have access into our lives to be able to aid us. We must free ourselves from all the clutter of fear, anger, hatred, envy and all traits that hinder our mind to think clearly, and we must replace it with growth-developing faith, hope, courage and care.

Seek help whenever necessary. Keep in mind that Divine intervention or human assistance always comes to people with a good purpose.

One time, I heard about a grandmother whose house was gutted by fire. Her house was located in a depressed area of a city, which was a rather crowded place with narrow alleys, making it difficult for fire trucks to go through. The fire broke out in one of the neighbouring houses due to an overheated electric fan. It was a hot summer day, and it happened when she wasn't at home.

From a distance, she could hear and see fire trucks responding in the direction where she lives. Suddenly, fear gripped her. She frantically rushed home. She was right. Her house was on fire along with the other houses. She had two grandchildren whom she left with her neighbor, but luckily they were able to escape unhurt.

When interviewed by a news reporter, she cried terribly about losing her house. To make things worst, she wasn't able to save anything at all, and this had been her fourth fire. "Tough luck," said the reporter. But then when she was asked if anybody in her family had been hurt or had perished in any of those four fires, her tears of sadness changed to tears of joy. All of a sudden she realized that, in spite of having experienced four fires, nobody had ever died or had been hurt in her family. Realizing this, she became grateful and thankful.

This grandmother came to realize that, despite the setback, she was actually a lucky lady, a demonstration of how the mind works in a negative state compared to a mind enlightened by a positive approach. So if your goal seems to be on fire and is burning to the ground, get a candle and light it from the fire. Keep that candle lit—you're going to need it to continue your journey to your goal realization.

Obstacles, problems, troubles or setbacks can be blessings in disguise. Remember that, in terms of accountability, we unconsciously co-create these scenarios to make us stronger. Consider this scenario: Two new drivers have just learned how to drive a car. One driver drives along a straight path, while the other drives down a zig-zag road. After having driven a number of miles, they have both gained more experience. But who became the better driver? It's easy to see that the one who traveled the road of obstacles, the zig-zag road, was the better driver in the end.

Come back to your goal after a setback. Draw lessons from these problems so that you can become a better person for next time. Like we mentioned earlier in this chapter, we draw lessons from history by learning from our mistakes and the mistakes of others. We need to learn to turn disadvantages to advantages. To turn a gloom into a bloom.

Remember that your mind is a very powerful tool. Use it the way it was designed to work: positively, wisely and intelligently.

GOALS THAT CARE

The word *care* has many definitions as well as many meanings. Care can mean looking after or providing for someone. It can also mean worry or a troubled state of mind about doing something properly. Or it can mean paying close attention, being heedful of, liking something, giving protection or taking responsibility. And it can also mean a feeling of concern or love. The last meaning is the type of care that we need to infuse into our goals.

Care is a strong word when it comes to human characteristics, so strong that it can move mountains, so to speak. It can drive a tough, heartless, no-nonsense guy to tears even if he is not the recipient of the care being given. Even in a world where the law of self-preservation prevails, people can usually see past the motive of a goal or project if proper care is injected into it, and the results are always favorable to all concerned. Even those who are not directly concerned with the "care project," when they learn about it through some form of media, would comment that it is a worthwhile project worthy of emulation. Human nature has a way of reciprocating kindness or care by giving it their full support when they see a worthy cause at work. Sometimes it can even turn rivals into friends, earning each other's mutual admiration because they can see and feel the care being put into the project.

When we focus on a goal with a touch of care, it is that care that serves as the catalyst that drives us to make this goal succeed. We get so excited that we cannot wait for it to materialize. The result will give us an air of satisfaction and contentment, so we can't wait to achieve it.

In an overall context, when care is part of everything we do, it leaves a lasting impression on the person receiving it. Even if the receiver unintentionally or effortlessly thinks about it, the effect lingers for a very long period of time. And care usually multiplies all by itself because beneficiaries or recipients cannot help but talk about it with other people. It's practically a word-of-mouth advertisement.

For example, I had the opportunity to visit Peru a few years ago and was deeply saddened and moved by the condition of many of the animals I saw there. Dogs roamed the streets, most of them wild, mangy, ill and starving. In fact, one dog had such a severe tumour on its abdomen that its stomach dragged on the ground and was raw and full of infection. The Peruvian people, who often struggle for food themselves, were mostly just annoyed by these packs of dogs and threw rocks at them or hit them with sticks. In addition to feeling sad and frustrated by what I saw, I became motivated and inspired to do what I could to make a difference for those animals that were so far from my home and so far from the sanctuary that my own pets thrive in.

When I returned home, I posted on my Facebook that I was interested in gathering together a group of like-minded individuals who would commit to the common goal of changing the life of even one dog in Peru. In the end, not only did I gather a group together, but one person who responded said that they had a Canadian friend who lived in Chile and worked for a non-profit organization called Vets Without Borders, and she was sure that they would have some ideas about how we could help. Despite my very busy life and the busy lives of the people involved, we have managed to make two donations to Vets Without Borders and remain committed to continuing to support the work of Elena Garde in Chile. This experience reminded me that when people are truly committed to a goal, and even one that includes no direct gain to those involved, there still exists passion and a willingness to give time, energy and effort easily and joyfully when it's for a good cause.

Now, imagine a world dominated by people who care. For the sake of this example, let us say that half of life's problems are human-made, while the other half are natural. Now imagine further that half of the human-made problems are preventable. If all humans lived a life of care or concern, preventable human-made problems could be totally eradicated. Then, if half of the natural problems could likewise be prevented by people who cared enough to find ways to avert or reduce them, that would eliminate about 50 percent of the overall problems in the world. Isn't that a good bargain? Wouldn't life be that much better?

Everybody could use some care once in a while. It boosts spirits to a higher level. In terms of goal selection, care is a big factor, so much so that if it's incorporated into the choice of the goal that we intend to pursue, it will propel the goal to sure success.

A serve-all idea is a sure-win-for-all situation. It amplifies the benefits that can be derived from it. In fact, some of the current new-age thinkers and prophets of our modern age have said that as we draw nearer to December 21, 2012, we are not reaching the end of our world, but instead we are reaching a time of quickening, a time where time will speed up to the degree that our consciousness and thoughts will manifest even quicker into our reality. Because of that, we will need to be increasingly mindful to what we are "putting into the morphic field" as it will be manifesting faster and faster. These new-age thinkers and prophets say that the time of selfishness must come to an end if we are to survive as a planet and as a species. This is true not only for our fellow man but also for our planet.

Speaking of our planet, the environment is another factor that can affect our aim to goal realization. So just how is the issue of environment related to achieving a goal? One of the areas where goal selection could use a lot of attention and care is the environment. When goals are concerned with keeping the environment in its original beauty, people usually support and laud it. Even more so are the projects that restore parts of the severed environment to its original state. And an even higher level of support will come to projects that not only restore severed environments to their original state, but beautify more than they originally were.

Let us now look at another aspect of the environment. Goal realization is dependent on our mental attitudes, and the way we think can in turn be affected by our environmental conditions. In other words, environmental conditions around which the goal evolves plays a vital role in making that goal successful.

Let's face it: Some environments have a degree of hostility, man-made or natural, so we have to incorporate some precautionary measures into our goal realization to prevent unfavorable events from happening, events that may hamper or hinder the progress of our goal. Get to know your environment; notice what is happening on the planet and make adjustments whenever necessary. Ask around and be a good observer. The earlier you can pre-empt a condition, the better off you'll be. This will better the chance of your endeavour's success by cutting out wasted time and turning it to a more productive use.

Have you ever heard the advertisement: "The garbage you throw out inadvertently or carelessly will come back to you"? This ad used to be shown on television in Asia where some people disposed of their garbage carelessly, then paid for their carelessness during the rainy season. When the flood waters entered the households, so did the garbage. It was a message of concern from one of the government agencies, and it is very true.

You see, our planet cannot and does not complain. You won't hear a word of complaint from the Earth—unless, of course, you consider earthquakes, volcanoes and hurricanes to be "complaining"—so we must make it an obligation to ourselves to care for it as best we can. The condition of the environment may or may not affect us right now, but it will definitely affect the generations to come. And this state-of-affairs will be of vital importance to the goals of our children and our grandchildren.

Care—it's a strong word with a wide scope, from human characteristics to environmental concerns about our planet.

ENTHUSIASM DRIVES THE GOAL

If enthusiasm can be bought as an item from a store, do you think it will sell? And if it does, just how much are you willing to pay for it?

I believe your response will be: "You must be kidding. It'll be a sellout. The store might probably run out of stock, you'll have to wait in queue for a long time before you can get your order no matter the price."

Just how important is enthusiasm in goal realization in one's life? It is so important that it occupies one of the top slots in the list of elements needed for successful living. It is so important that it is one of the deciding factors to realize one's goal.

There is no doubt that everyone likes talking to enthusiastic people, unless a person likes to be in a gloomy state, which then manifests usually as the old adage "misery likes company.". Enthusiastic people keep the conversation alive and upbeat. You feel like you are partying. And when you feel like you're partying, you wish the night will never end.

Imagine yourself in the middle of an argument or a debate between two opposing sides on an issue. When the mood gets rough, and even when you are not in a bad mood at first, you get to feel rough and in an argumentative mood. Your mood swings in accordance to the situation. It is like when you hear a song you like, you feel like singing along. And that mood will usually prevail for quite a while long after you've left the scene where it took place and it will only change when something else prevails over it.

Imagine yourself in the middle of a discussion with enthusiastic people. Even if you are not the enthusiastic type, you begin to turn enthusiastic yourself. Even when you are not familiar with the topic at hand, your tendency is to be inquisitive and you keep asking questions. The more questions you ask, the more alive the conversation gets. And you get to learn more, broadening your knowledge on certain issues. Quite educational, isn't it?

Enthusiasm brings out the hyper character in us. It is like adding more wood to a bonfire making you feel like you want to roast marshmallows in it. Honestly, as I am writing this, I'm beginning to feel more enthusiastic myself.

The point is that enthusiasm is contagious like a disease. This is one contagious disease that has a desirable effect. As a matter of fact, enthusiasm is the only disease that everybody wants to contract. If there is a category in the Guinness Book of World Records for being the contagious disease most people would like to have with them, it is enthusiasm. Law enforcers would probably ban the quarantine of this disease.

Now, just how do you get enthusiastic, especially when your surroundings, the weather condition and the general situation feels down and out?

Here are some helpful tips to develop enthusiasm:

Adopt the "as if" principle. It is believed that this was first stated by Professor William James, at times known as the father of American Psychological Science. This is an effective time- and people-tested principle.

Consider this scenario: Let's say you frequently or almost always see a particular actor play the role of a comedian in movies and television shows. You would then always identify or equate this actor with comedy even if he is not even funny in real life. The good news is that the actor himself may also feel the effects of being in a laughing mood most of the time, even if his life is full of dramatic experiences. Ultimately, this actor may wind up being a happy person simply because of his role, a confirmation that laughter is the best medicine. If he portrays other types of roles, he seems to be out of place to you since you're just not used to seeing him play roles other than a comedian.

At one time or another in your childhood years, I believe you've come across superhero characters in comic books or magazines. And I believe that you've imagined yourself to be like these superheroes, saving people from disastrous situations or winning over the bad guys. This is an "as if" principle in fantasized form. Do you remember?

I would suggest at this point that you try to apply the "as if" principle with someone near or beside you to confirm its effectiveness. Think creatively.

Another similar principle is the "what if." If you are in the business of developing products of specialized use, you are most likely exposed to a lot of experimentation. When you come up with an idea on a product you'd like to try, even if the idea seems unconventional, would you try it? Would you be saying to yourself: "What if I try to..."?

Adapt enthusiasm into the "practice makes perfect" principle. In other words, be enthusiastic about almost everything you do everyday no matter how insignificant they are, no matter how small they are. All those small things, when added up, become big. This is the "as if" principle in small ways.

You are probably also familiar with the expression: "Beauty is in the eye of the beholder." Even if a sight, a scene, or anything does not look too beautiful or enthusiastic, try to see its beauty and be enthusiastic about it. On the not-so-beautiful side, try to be enthusiastic in finding ways to improve it.

As you wake up each morning, be enthusiastic about the things you are going to do that day. Bring enthusiasm to even your routine morning chores like taking a shower, getting dressed, eating breakfast, taking the bus or driving your car (even in heavy traffic), in the office, and all the way up to the time when you reach home for dinner and until you go to bed, enthusiastically looking forward to tomorrow—remember our suggestion earlier about having your fall-asleep thought be a gratitude thought.

In the course of the day, you may experience non-enthusiastic traits from other people. Don't get carried away and don't be as non-enthusiastic as they are. Instead, show enthusiasm to these people and they may become enthusiastic too because of you. Lead, don't just follow. That will give you the feeling of you setting a good example for the benefit of all. There are studies that support the idea that when people are in a room together for at least 15 minutes, the vibrational energies in the room will synchronize and they will synchronize to the highest level that is in the space.

GOAL ACHIEVERS

Achievement assumes many faces. How will you rate yourself once you have achieved your goal?

"Achievers One" are achievers who have accumulated fame and fortune but remain unhappy in spite of it. It sounds logical but illogical as well. They have reached the top of their career, the pinnacle of their goal, but they somehow remain unhappy. They may have everything, but the feeling of emptiness looms heavy in their hearts. Perhaps along the way, they have neglected to look after the welfare of their fellow man, or worse, may have used their fellow man to their personal advantage. They may be aware that they did not give their best performance yet still got to the top, a feeling of "I don't deserve all this" or "I'd rather be poor and happy than rich but unhappy."

"Achievers Two" are achievers who have consolidated everything they have acquired in the course of their endeavour to a rather small in size but vast reservoir of knowledge: their head. Sounds like the wrong place to keep an achievement. They boast about their achievement, drawing awe from people they come in contact with. They have virtually enslaved themselves to their achievement so that nothing else matters to them.

What then are real achievers made of? A real achiever is defined as one who:

- Is truly happy and contented with the result or outcome of the goal s/he has aimed to attain no matter how small it is.
- In spite the contentment, continues to further improve his/her skill and knowledge.
- Aims for excellence and makes it a limitless endeavour.
- Remains steadfast and humble or even humbler that s/he used to be in spite of his/her achievement.
- Have served and will continue to serve his/her fellow man.
- Shares his/her talents with others in furtherance of improvement and development.
- Have not stepped on other's toes while in the pursuit of their goal.
- Who remain grateful to the people who have helped him/her attain success.
- Does not boast of their accomplishment.
- Have faith in both themselves and a higher power.

This seems to be a long list of criteria that is difficult to follow. Actually, it isn't. Only the achiever can confirm this through his/her honest feeling of how the events led to their success. It is a feeling that no exact word will suffice to describe it, though the closest is perhaps gratefulness.

Grateful achievers keep an open mind focused on returning favours they received, not necessarily to the ones who one way or another have contributed to their success, but also to persons unknown to them so long as they see that such persons are truly in need of help in their struggle to succeed. These achievers see themselves in the shoes of the striving persons when they were still striving, and they know how it feels to encounter difficulties along the way.

Helping others, one of the main things in achievers, makes life easier for all of us. There is no point in making life difficult for each other. It's just a waste of time.

Actions like this have a multiplicity effect that contributes to the progress of the nation as a whole. Just like enthusiasm, helping each other is contagious. Because of achievers, what started as a seed is now a tree. No matter how small the help of one person is, it contributes to the success of a nation. Each achiever becomes an asset to his/her community. This is the stuff great communities are made of. Wouldn't you want to be part of it?

AGELESS GOAL

Age need not be a deterrent to the pursuit of your goal, nor should it hamper your enthusiasm in furtherance to continue improvement or excellence of it. As a matter of fact, we can even start venturing on new ideas. Starting young or not so young in aiming for a goal is practically negligible that it makes no difference. What matters is your attitude towards your aim and that it be positive.

Growing old is all in the mind, but only if we let it be. Yes, it's visible when we grow old, but these changes are only on our physique. Our actions and reflexes may be slower than before. Our hair may be thinner and gray. Our skin may be dry and wrinkled. But our mind and spirit will remain young and vibrant as ever, even wiser than ever.

Only the physical side of us gets old, the mental and spiritual sides are as young as ever. Age or aging, as defined in the dictionary, is synonymous to growing old. "Growing" is a progressive word, so there is every reason for us to go with the flow, to be optimistic.

With age comes wisdom, maturity and experience. How we choose to mature depends on how we think of ourselves. If we think we are non-productive, worn-out and ruggedly unattractive, ridden with health problems, then we will be what we think we are. However, if we welcome age with a positive outlook, having emerged a wiser and more experienced person, full of wisdom and vitality in spite of age, then this chapter of our life will bring even more excitement, like looking forward to sharing our experiences with our grandchildren, the younger generation. What we choose to be, we will be. Only we can control ourselves. I see no reason why we would choose to be gloomy, feeling self-pity and being unproductive in senior age when we have the option to emerge bright and upbeat.

Share experiences with the younger generation. Tell them both the good ones and even the not-so-good ones. Both ways, they will draw lessons from them. We are, in essence, a living history library that they can research from, being able to answer their inquisitive questions in person, sharing experiences which are far better that machine-produced information. And you know what makes our information unique compared to machine-produced ones? It can be filled with emotion and excitement. That will surely draw a "cool" comment from youngsters. One of the things that has historically drawn me to aboriginal culture is the focus on the respect of their "elders." I believe we have moved away from some of this ideology and also believe we could learn from those cultures and see the value in reintroducing that collective value back into our communities.

When we have grandchildren and they start to call us grandpa or grandma, how we react to it is entirely up to us. It's a choice between the sound of useless, cranky, good-for-nothing, step-aside grandpa or grandma; or the sound of fun-filled, welcome, looking-forward-to, sunshine-drenched grandpa or grandma. What will your choice be?

I would like to use this space to leave a message to the children and grandchildren of seniors. Picture yourselves when you become grandparents someday. Would you like to be left alone living by yourselves, sent off to senior homes, feeling lonely and desolate, taken for granted as if you don't exist anymore? Or do you want to be riddled with questions from wide-eyed children, running like a child as if childhood came the second time around (not the mental second-childhood stuff), walking hand-in-hand with your loved ones on a flower-filled countryside and simply being happy? You can make a difference on how seniors feel.

Growing old can be rewarding.

FINALIZING THE GOAL

In this final section on goal realization, I would like to impart disciplines to you that will serve as guidelines to goal realization. I believe you will find them very useful as they did to others. Some of them have been mentioned earlier, most others will be mentioned as we go along.

To pursue our goal, we need to have:

• A sound mind with an absolute positive attitude

• A healthy body

• A sense of faith.

How do we initiate the process of goal realization?

Deep within us is an inherent God-given skill that we need to call up and bring into the open. This skill cannot deliver positive results until we have polished it to its full potential. It takes hard work and dedication to turn it into a workable, efficient machine that will deliver results aimed at the goal we envision to achieve.

Focused work which is reflective of all the positive attitudes we have earlier discussed will serve as the backbone in building our goal. Despite all the hardships that we will encounter, we must stand firm and emerge victorious, and stop at nothing until we have our goal at hand.

Ask yourself these questions:

- Have I reached my full potential in life?
- Am I really satisfied with the way I am?
- Have I achieved anything in life so far?
- Have I contributed to the well-being of my fellow man?
- Am I an asset to society?
- Am I really happy?

A "No" answer to most of the questions should encourage us to aim for our goal.

The following disciplines can serve as guidelines:

Feel in your heart and mind the goal you love or want to attain.

Feel and search within your heart and mind the kind of things you love to do and have the skill or know-how in doing them. When you follow your heart and mind's desires, you have gained your first step towards goal realization. You will always be enthusiastic about it and this gives you an advantage. Doing something you are familiar with and love to do will make things easier to accomplish so there will be lesser obstacles. Even in the absence of things needed to realize a goal you love to pursue, you will somehow exhaust all the means to make it come true. This trait is inherent within us. A rather simple example is that say you want to see a concert of your favourite band group but don't have enough cash to spend for it—you'll try to save from other less important expenses.

In the event you cannot feel in your heart and mind the goal you want to pursue, here's a simple rule that you can follow: "Find a need and fill it." These words, credited to the great industrialist Henry Kaiser, have been the guiding principle of many successful entrepreneurs.

Hone your thinking.

Hone or sharpen your thinking. Distinguish short-term, medium-term, and long-term goals. See if the short-term goal will benefit your medium-term goal, which in turn can be an advantage for your long-term goal. Keep them co-related as much as possible. Know the capacity you can handle. Be fantastic but be realistic. When you set the plan, timetable and scope, try to envision in your mind the sequence of events that are probable to happen, how to go about it, possible solutions to obstacles, right approach to situations, among others.

Aim for the best result.

Whatever outcome comes out of your quest to pursue your goal, make sure you do your best. This will eliminate saying to yourself: "if only I did my best" in case things turn out second best or third best, or worse, a total failure. However, don't stop if it's a failure. Capitalize by drawing a lesson or two from it so that you won't commit the same mistake when you do it again. "Next time, it will be ..." is what you must say to yourself. This kind of experience will make you a more skillful, knowledgeable and learned person.

Differentiate goals from wishes.

Wishes are daydreams or fantasies of what you want to achieve in life, but if they're not acted upon, will remain as fantasies and never turn to realistic goals. To achieve your goal, you have to act, move and work hard at it. Make a definite plan and timetable to reach the ultimate result. Life is not a garden or a bed of roses ready for us to pick and enjoy. You have to plant them, nurture them constantly, water them, give them enough sunshine, fertilize them, talk to them if you have to and harvest them by the time the roses are in full bloom.

To achieve your primary goal, you may need secondary goals.

Sometimes, success in goal realization may seem beyond reach. There seems to be an overwhelming gap in-between. Be that as it may, don't let that discourage you. Take it as a challenge to your intelligence. You may need secondary goals as stepping stones to your primary goal, a bridge to connect the gap. It is like taking several flights from different airlines to different places until you finally reach your intended destination. In this case, you may even have to mix air travel with sea and land travel.

Focus on goals that will benefit others as well.

Your goal may be self-serving, but more so, it must benefit as many people as possible. Compared to a self-centered goal, which restricts the flow of success, a serve-all goal releases an aura of confidence and trust gained from other people. Let's face it, people can somehow see through you if your intention is self-serving or all-serving.

Attempt to aim for a goal that will make you an asset to society, a goal that people will appreciate what you contribute. Goals that will make life easier, goals that will make people smile, goals that will make this world a better place to live in, now and for generations to come.

Be humble every step of the way in achieving your goal.

For every secondary goal you achieve, exercise humility. Never be boastful of your small goals. Never brag about small goals and tell people you are sure to achieve your ultimate goal because of your small successes. I am not discouraging you to aim for your ultimate goal. In fact, the more I am encouraging you to go forth and do it with all humility. As we all know, humility is a virtue and a goal graced with virtue is sure to succeed.

Whenever you set to realize a goal, you must hold on to it tenaciously. Make your goal as clear and as vivid as you can.

By the time you have achieved your goal, you will feel an air of satisfaction, contentment; to be exact, it is a feeling of happiness. Doesn't this feeling turn the "No" answers to our earlier questions to "Yes"?

Let us go back to these questions.

- Have I reached my full potential in life? *Yes, I have.*

- Am I really satisfied with the way I am? *I am now.*

- Have I achieved anything in life so far? *Yes, I have.*

- Have I contributed to the well-being of my fellow man? *I firmly believe I do.*

- Am I an asset to society? *I believe I am.*

- Am I really happy? *Yes, I am.*

And you know what's good about achieving your goal aside from happiness?

You will feel an air of confidence, self-esteem and respect for yourself, so that you can't help but congratulate yourself. You will be stronger not only mentally but spiritually as well, and in the long run you have moved that much closer to an inspired life and having successfully rewritten those old beliefs and attitudes that never really served you in the long run anyhow.

Chapter Nine:
Faith

Whenever we hear or talk about prayer, we equate the word with God. Prayer is the means of communication between man and his Creator. It is the medium by which man transmits his intentions to God.

All over the world, people of different races, beliefs and cultures embrace different religions. Depending on the country, some religions may be more dominant than others. I don't want to spend time debating religion, but this chapter is devoted to the concept of faith and I wouldn't be able to speak about faith without including some reference to spirituality.

We cannot discount that there are a few of us who doubt that a higher power exists. To this end, I will refer to that higher power as "Spirit" so as to honour the many types of spirituality that exist on the planet. I will also interchange between "He" and "She" in honour of my belief that God has no gender, is pure and formless and not bound by the limitations of gender.

I think at one time or another, it has occurred to all of us to try to find answers to questions such as:

- How did life originate?
- Where did the Earth and the universe and everything in them come from?
- Who made them?
- In short, who started all of these?

Personally, I think we will not find the answers if we stick to our sense of reasoning on natural laws even if we live nine lives. That leaves us only one option: The Great Spirit started all these.

The wonderful thing about these creations, living or otherwise and including us, is that they are all unique. Even identical twins are not alike. No one thing is an exact replica of the other. DNA proves this. So it doesn't matter what religion you're in. The important thing is that you have spiritual faith.

Studies have shown that having this kind of faith actually prolongs your life. The inner peace that your faith brings can contribute significantly to good mental and emotional health. If you have spiritual faith, you have the power to conquer all obstacles that come along the way.

In the context of inspiration and conquering fear, prayer and faith play the most important parts. Taking prayer and faith away from the pursuit of an inspired life is like taking the spine away from a human body—everything collapses. The importance of prayer and faith cannot be overstated.

Inspiration originates from an idea, while an idea originates from our mind. What originates from our mind—independent of our belief system—originates from Spirit, what some may call our Higher Self. Since Spirit is the original source of our idea to set an achievable goal, it is natural that we ask Spirit, or our Higher Self, to guide us in our pursuit, to aid us in times of need, and that we thank Spirit for our every success, no matter how big or small, and we offer back to Spirit whatever we have accomplished. And the medium we can use to have access to Spirit is through prayer or meditation.

When two or more people want to discuss something, they talk to each other through their lips and listen with their ears, with the brain acting as the central processing unit. It's slightly different when we communicate with Spirit through prayers or quiet contemplation, telling Him our personal intentions. We do the talking, Spirit does the listening. We tell Her our problems or intentions. He listens and finds solutions or answers to them. He acts and tells us His responses through our thoughts and our minds. The rest is up to us.

Sometimes, two people argue because of their differences in opinion. Again with Spirit, it is slightly different—She won't complain like we usually do, nor argue with us even if we pour out our aches and pains to Him and start to blame Her for all these misgivings. He will just stay silent, listening and waiting until we come back to our senses. One way or the other, He knows we will. Once our senses are back on track, He will start to work through our thoughts, just like before, and let us know what we need to know.

As long as our intentions are attuned to things that will bring good not only to us but also to our neighbors, we can expect full support from Spirit.

Remember that we need Spirit in our lives. In return, She responds to our needs as proof of His love for us. With this in mind, whenever we approach Him, be honest and sincere. Approach Her with a humble and contrite heart.

I used to wonder why prayers are repeated many times over. Over and over again, day after day, week after week, and so on—it's always the same prayers. I said "used to" because I believe that I've found the answer. I don't know if you'll agree with me, but I'll share it with you anyway.

A prayer is actually an affirmation: it is said repeatedly not for Spirit's benefit, but for our own. Spirit wants to instill in us the value and habit of practice. As we all know, practice makes perfect. She uses prayers as an instrument of forming this habit of practice in us. The question is "what for"?

By practicing positive attitudes in life over and over again, we may ultimately develop these attitudes and keep them in us for good. It's like learning to drive a car: You get to be a good driver only through practice.

If we want to instill the positive values and attitudes needed for inspiration but find it difficult to start doing so, it will even be more difficult to sustain it over time; but either way, the only way to do it is through practice. This is tantamount to conditioning our mind, body and spirit into this habit. Once we are used to it, it will remain in us for good.

At times, we have problems that overwhelm us and approach Spirit for help, but He seems to be nowhere in sight; at these times, we feel like Spirit is neglecting us. We begin to shy away from Her and start to blame Her for all the problems we have. It's as if we have built a wall separating Spirit from us. When other people notice this condition in us and we tell them the reason why, they say: "Spirit has His reasons. She knows what is best for us." However, we are not convinced.

This has some similarity to the story "Footprints in the Sand," if you're familiar with it. In the story, a man walking on the beach could see two sets of footprints on the sand during his good times. One set belonged to the man, the other to the Lord. During the bad times, the man could see only one set of footprints and he would wonder why the Lord would abandon him during his lowest moments in life. The Lord replied: "I would never leave you. Every time you see only one set of footprints, it was then that I carried you."

Here is some food for thought and soul, which I believe is the reasons why Spirit is silent to our problems (some of the answers are in the form of questions that reflects back to us):

1. Did I approach Spirit without a ready pre-condition? Is it possible that I told myself: "If Spirit does not help me on this, I will lose faith in Him. It's His loss, not mine." Understanding how the law of attraction truly works, what may I have just set up in that moment?

2. If Spirit acted favorably to solve my problem, will His actions make me a stronger person? Or perhaps learning to own and stand in my own power would be the greatest gift that Spirit could give me?

Remember that prayer and meditation is the ultimate solution to our troubles and problems. It is how we connect to our Intuition, our "Know I Know." Prayers should not be our last resort if we encounter difficulties—they should be our first.

Make it a habit to pray or meditate to and with Spirit, not only during bad times but also during simple times. Treat Spirit as your friend and ally in the journey of inspiration.

I would like to end this chapter with some teachings from the Hawaiian Islands, knowledge referred to as Kahuna. These wisdom teachings can simply help anchor you and teach you how to hold faith and, more importantly, have a positive outlook on life and its possibilities. It should sum up all that we have learned on this journey together.

Kahuna is not an occult system but is actually based on human psychology. Huna, as it's also known, simply emphasizes basic, normal living in every aspect of life. It's a day-to-day road-map for traveling through life.

The basic beliefs of Huna can actually be summed up in two simple ideas: "no hurt, no sin"—"sin" being defined as causing harm to yourself or hurting another person. And the other is that you must "serve to deserve." This means that you must be of help to others in order to feel worthy of goodness in your own life. I believe so strongly in these principles that a fundamental part of our program in Personal Best was tailored to include elements of service to others. I have observed over and over again the increase in my participants ability to feel joy and happiness when they have had the experience of service to and with others.

Believers of Huna are taught that the human being consists of: the body, the mind—which encompasses the conscious (uhane: the middle self) and the subconscious (unihipili: low self)—and the aumakua, the super conscious, or high self. The concept of a deity was considered one step above the high self and is actually believed to be a part of the human personality; we have a Divine connection. Hence we see a link here to the mind, body and spirit connection that many doctrines refer to.

Believers use the triangular symbol to denote that, once we have all aspects of the triad which is us working in harmony, we are in perfect communication. All the selves must do their separate jobs and work together in order to achieve our potential as humans and spiritual beings. When they are out of balance, our results are also out of balance.

When all three are working harmoniously together to solve a problem in the here and now and are geared towards creating a future of beauty and power, good things begin to happen, and it may appear to be a miracle both to you and to others in your life. Believers, however, do not believe that this is in any way super-natural, but simply the natural order of things working as they are supposed to work; hence it leaves space for nothing more complicated than faith that all is in divine and perfect order. Conceptually, then, we understand that we are the source and cause; life is not happening to us, but rather it is happening through us. If we understand that completely, then we recognize that we can create anything we desire and that we don't have to wait for a gift from Spirit, or be angry at Spirit when what we say we want does not manifest. We honour our part in all aspects of our creation energy and in all aspects of how we create our results.

1. EKE': THE WORLD IS WHAT YOU THINK IT IS

Everything in our world, everything in our own reality, comes from our thoughts. We share this with friends, family, co-workers and everyone else. According to the Huna belief, if we want to change our world, we must first change our thoughts. It is a waste of time and energy to try and change the outer world on our own. We must begin by changing ourselves if we wish to help change the world. It begins with us. It honours that we only have control over three things and three things only—how we think, feel and act. So to change what we are doing, especially those things that cause us pain or suffering, we must understand that their origins are in our thinking as all behaviour stems from our thoughts. My inner world creates my other world. This is Eke' working within to create the outer world. All the other principles of Huna stem from this one.

2. KALA: WE ARE ALL CONNECTED; THERE IS NO SEPARATION AND NO LIMITS

Everything in the universe is connected. Our minds and bodies are connected, as well as Earth to man, plants, animals, sky and ocean. We are all connected and the separation we perceive is merely an illusion. It's only our thoughts that make us believe that we are separate from the rest. According to the Huna belief, this causes suffering in humankind. Underneath this sense of separation is the connection. If we rid ourselves of these thoughts of separateness, we will reconnect and become one again, and be healed. If you have ever been to Hawaii, you may have heard the locals use the phrase "hang loose," which simply means that when you get uptight, you create a tension, which in turn causes the separation. But when you "hang loose," you relax, you feel better, your relationships become better and you go with the flow. Kala does not mean that you must accept things as they are, only that if you relax with them, you can then react in a way that does not create further suffering by attracting more of it into your life. In fact, author and speaker Gregg Braden, in his book *The God Code*, teaches us that there is scientific evidence to support that we are in fact made of God. For example, the name Ya' Hweh, which is Hebrew for the word God, corresponds with the building blocks of DNA. He suggests that if that is evidence we are "of" God, then we would understand we are all conceptually one; and if we are all one, then faith comes from knowing that we are in no way, shape or form alone in this journey we call life.

3. MAKEA: ENERGY FLOWS WHERE ATTENTION GOES

Events are created wherever there is a flow of energy and attention. Focusing your attention on a particular object or idea causes the energy to flow in that direction. Whatever the nature of your thoughts is, you feel that flow in return. Positive energy put out into the universe means positive energy flowing back to you. The same goes for negative energy: If you put negative energy out into the universe, it will return to you as well. If you put out thoughts of abundance, not occasionally but consistently, then abundance flows back to you. You can develop the skill that will begin to bring the positive energy back into your life. Do not focus on anger or fear, but on happiness and joy. Change your attention and you change your world. This is the fundamental principle behind step two of the Law of Attraction, which states that after you have set your intention, you must put energy and attention toward what your intention is. If do not focus energetically, the "order" is lost in the Universe and will not manifest. It is also why many people who have a tremendous amount of negative self talk have problems with self confidence and self esteem and will go as far as to attract people into their life that confirm what they have been thinking.

4. MANOUA: NOW IS THE TIME OF POWER

This is to teach you to remain in the moment. There is no power in the past and no power in the future. There is only power in this moment, right now. The past has no power over you unless you allow it; you cannot change your past, but by not focusing on it, you give it no energy, and without energy, the past loses its power over you. Whatever thoughts you possess are what you will bring with you into this moment. Your thoughts are creating your reality. So if you have beauty in your life, you will create beauty. And you must increase that beauty by appreciating it right now. If you stop appreciating the beauty, you will lose your sense of beauty and it will disappear from your life. Appreciating what's around you causes it to increase. The more you take pleasure in what's around you, the stronger it becomes. According to the Huna belief, the future does not lay waiting for you to move forward and run into it. It is created in every present moment by what you think right now. Completing issues from the past leaves a space for a clean, powerful future.

5. ALOHA: LOVE, PURE AND SIMPLE

The root of the word means, "to be happy with." The secret here is that to love is to be happy with something or someone. The degree of your happiness dictates the degree to which you are in love. The feeling of love is important, and the expression of it also has significance. Letting criticism, anger, and unhappiness in will diminish that love and cause pain around you. Love does not mean inflicting pain, hurting people, or getting yourself hurt. Love means embracing the happiness, the joy and the pleasure in any relationship and leaving a space of forgiveness for the mistakes all humans make at various points in their lives.

6. MANA: DIVINE, CREATIVE POWER OR LIFE FORCE

This belief presupposes that there is only one source of power and that the source flows through each of us on the planet. It flows not only through human beings, but through the Earth and everything that lives on it or above it. Mana is considered the inner power that gives each thing its own creativity. Mana is the power of the sea and the wind through the clouds. It is the power of human beings to be creative and to be the creator. Conceptually, you must understand that power comes through you, and if that is true you will also understand that nothing outside of you has any power over you. Your very existence stems from this power within, and if you believe that something else has any real power over you, it diminishes your own power and leaves you vulnerable to be a victim. In this book, we have spent significant time understanding the draining energy that comes with the experience of victimization. Holding it back, playing small or pretending you don't have the power also diminishes it. By allowing yourself to experience this power, to feel it, to use it and claim it, gives you the power to reach your highest potential and to take the actions necessary to manifest and magnetize your dreams.

7. PONO: EFFECTIVENESS IS THE MEASURE OF TRUTH

There is no one way to do anything. There is always an alternative. We are not stuck doing things one way forever. There is no one truth, or one method or technique. There is no one kind of medicine or one way to be happy. The ways you can use to achieve your goals and attain happiness are myriad. And nothing is carved in stone. If you feel like you only have one choice in a situation, then you will often feel like there is rigidity in the space, and when it feels rigid, resistance follows. When you feel like you only have two choices, you may feel like you have dilemma, and this does not usually feel powerful and feels more like a lesser-of-two-evils way to choose. However, if you believe that there are multiple choices in terms of how to respond to things in your life, then you feel you have flexibility. Being flexible means being powerful. So your purpose or plan may be of paramount importance, but the methods to achieving them are vast. Use the proper means to achieve the goal. For instance, if what you desire is peace, you must use peaceful means to achieve that goal and knowing that there are many faces of peace, you can test and re-test to see what is working for you. Most would agree that violence is inappropriate, because it usually only attracts a violent response. According to this principle of Huna, if you start out with peace in your heart, you will move towards peace in your life. This principle is a practical truth and may be used as a way of living with others and yourself.

According to well-known Huna researcher Max Freedom Long, "If you are not using Huna, you are working too hard."

Conclusion

Before we end, let me ask you a simple question. It's not an overly complicated question, but a question none the less. What do Superman, Spiderman, Batman, the X-men and the Incredible Hulk have in common? Yes, they all have supernatural powers—special abilities that make them supreme, invincible and indestructible, and which cause them to be recognized as superheroes. Yes, they use their supernatural powers to do good things to and for people and defeat evil. But, unfortunately, they are not real. They are only constructs of man's creative imagination. They don't exist in reality. That's why, unlike in comic books and movies, when our city is in trouble, there's no superhero to call to save the day. It really seems to be too good to be true, doesn't it?

Now, let's try to add another one in the list, but this time it's a real person, say you, or me, or your teacher, or my next-door neighbor, or simply anyone who exists in this world. The list would now be like this: Superman, Spiderman, Batman, the X-men, the Incredible Hulk and you. Again, same question: What is the common factor among those in the list? Remember, that includes you now.

So before answering, you might ask another question first: "Is there really something that we all possess?" Indeed, there is. Even changing the last entry to me, your teacher, my next-door neighbor or whatever other real person you may think of, there will always be something in common between a superhero and a real person like you and me—and that something is power.

Have you ever envied a superhero for having supernatural powers? I think we all have. Just imagine how amazing and fascinating it would be to become invisible even for just a minute or two, to fly across mountains and seas, to climb tall buildings and walls, to create fire or ice depending on what the situation needs, or to simply have the physical strength to be able to do things that normal people can't. But are these kinds of powers the only way to make us superior over others?

As real people in the real world, we can never possess any of these supernatural physical powers. What we do have, however, is the power to mold our personality, to shape our future, to create our destiny and to determine who and what we are—a power greater than any other supernatural powers; a power that builds reality and not mere imagination; a power which everyone possesses and can make themselves into a hero in their own ways. This is the power of your mind and is what this whole journey has been about, understanding why we do what we do, consciously and less than consciously.

Funny how we tend to be so addicted in looking outside ourselves that we have almost totally lost access to our inner being. We are so afraid to look inward because we might not be happy with what we could see. We make our lives so hectic that we eliminate the slightest risk of looking into ourselves. Therefore, we settle on observing things outside of our own. We make comparisons, judgments and evaluations, which only leads us to concluding, and worse accepting the fact, that we are inferior to others.

What we have forgotten (and I hope you have learned) is that we have the power to reverse what the outside world makes us believe in. If it says that we are wrong, then we have the power to make us right. If it says we are losers, we have the power to be winners. If it says we are non-existent, we have the power to make everyone see that we are alive and surviving. And that is how the power of our mind works—making us more supreme, invincible and indestructible than any other superhero.

If the world says you can't, then say "I can. Therefore, I will."

"People spend a lifetime searching for happiness and looking for peace. They chase idle dreams, addictions, religions, even other people, hoping to fill the emptiness that plagues them. The irony is the only place they ever needed to search was within," said author and speaker Ramona Anderson.

Almost all people long and seek for well-being, contentment and a state of tranquility that we call happiness and inspiration. The search for inspiration starts and ends within us. In all of these concerns, at the end of it all, one Great Question exists: What, then, was the purpose of life?

"The purpose of life is the expansion of happiness," according to the creator of Transcendental Meditation, Maharishi Yogi. If we stop and think about it clearly, the purpose of life is to be happy. From the very heart of our being, we simply desire complete and lasting happiness. This does not only mean we should be contented with life, but we must also appreciate life itself. It is also important to discover what will bring about the greatest degree of happiness.

So in summary, here are the 10 keys to happiness and to having inspiration:

1. Learn to appreciate simple things and manage desires.
2. Happiness is found within us. It is in the choices that we make.
3. Attitude, attitude, attitude! How we react and deal with life's challenges spell the difference between happiness and misery.
4. Happy feelings are results of happy thoughts.
5. Happiness is a way of life.
6. Happiness is mostly created and rarely given.
7. Learn to avoid or overcome factors that contribute to unhappiness.

8. We take accountability for our own happiness.

9. Happiness is enhanced by feelings of love and appreciation!

10. Happy people celebrate and appreciate life every day. Happiness is theirs for keeps.

Savour the beauty of life! Live to the fullest! Make each day a happy day and enjoy your journey to an inspired life!

In gratitude and in Spirit,

Rae-ann

ABOUT THE AUTHOR

Personal development has not just been a part of Rae-ann's life, it has been the driving force behind her life. Her desire to raise the consciousness of humanity and make a difference has been the fuel of her existence. She does this through coaching, facilitating seminars, designing workshops and is currently learning to lead the sacred ceremony of a sweatlodge.

Her training in psychology, hypnotherapy, NLP and Shamanic Coaching make her approach to healing and growing eclectic and if nothing else interesting for those she works with. When she is not working she enjoys spending time in nature.

Her home is a beautiful log house, situated on 7 acres near Sherwood Park, Alberta. She has a beautiful siberian husky named Aurora, a miniature donkey who she affectionately calls Donkey and a beautiful red dunn horse she calls Handsome; balancing out the tribe are her cats Frank and Rosie. In addition to the four-legged creatures, she shares her home with her partner Jeff and currently only has one of her children, Kenny, still residing with her.

If you are interested in working with her you can reach her at rae-ann@creatorscode.com.